JUMBLE

Genius

Do You Have Puzzle Smarts?

Henri Arnold, Bob Lee,
and Mike Argirion

TRIUMPH
B O O K S
CHICAGO

This book is available in quantity at special discounts
for your group or organization.

For further information, contact:

Triumph Books
542 South Dearborn Street
Suite 750
Chicago, Illinois 60605
(312) 939-3330
Fax (312) 663-3557

Printed in U.S.A.

ISBN-13: 978-1-57243-896-5
ISBN-10: 1-57243-896-7

Design by Sue Knopf

CONTENTS

JUMBLE Genius

Classic Puzzles

JUMBLE®

Unscramble these four Jumbles, one letter to
each square, to form four ordinary words.

NYSAP

FRACT

BUHLEM

BREMME

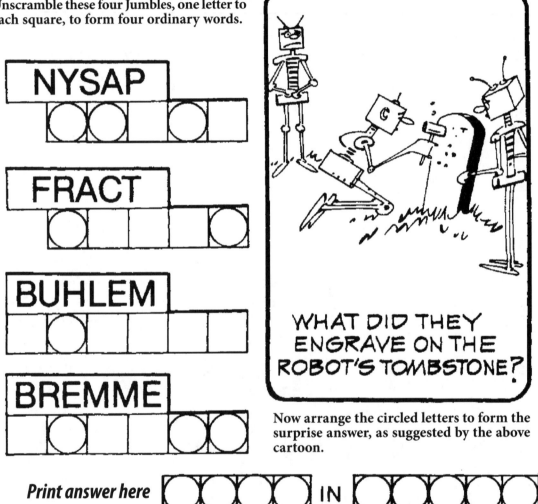

WHAT DID THEY
ENGRAVE ON THE
ROBOT'S TOMBSTONE?

Now arrange the circled letters to form the
surprise answer, as suggested by the above
cartoon.

Print answer here ⬡⬡⬡⬡⬡ IN ⬡⬡⬡⬡⬡⬡

JUMBLE®

Unscramble these four Jumbles, one letter to
each square, to form four ordinary words.

SASIB

PALLE

MERMAH

BOALIN

My client demands full
restitution for what
he wrote

OBLIGATED
ACCORDING TO
LAW WHEN YOU
"CONCOCT" A LIBEL.

Now arrange the circled letters to form the
surprise answer, as suggested by the above
cartoon.

Print answer here " ☐☐☐☐☐☐ "

JUMBLE®

Unscramble these four Jumbles, one letter to each square, to form four ordinary words.

ENFLO

AKNEW

WOAMED

ROHRRO

Where's that waiter? One minute he's here and the next he's gone!

PRESENT AT PRESENT BUT NOT PRESENT.

Now arrange the circled letters to form the surprise answer, as suggested by the above cartoon.

Print answer here " ⬡⬡⬡ – ⬡⬡⬡⬡ "

JUMBLE®

Unscramble these four Jumbles, one letter to each square, to form four ordinary words.

DEYNE

YURUS

ONCOMM

SHRAID

WHAT SHE TOLD HER COWBOY FRIEND NOT TO DO.

Now arrange the circled letters to form the surprise answer, as suggested by the above cartoon.

Print answer here

JUMBLE®

Unscramble these four Jumbles, one letter to
each square, to form four ordinary words.

GOWAN

NIYKK

LOICAS

BLOUED

WHAT HAPPENED
TO THE MAN
WHO INVENTED
VANISHING CREAM?

Now arrange the circled letters to form the
surprise answer, as suggested by the above
cartoon.

Print answer here

JUMBLE®

Unscramble these four Jumbles, one letter to
each square, to form four ordinary words.

KRIHE

LODOF

PANMEC

LEEXUD

WHAT SHE TOLD
HER HUSBAND HE
HAD BETTER DO
WHILE ON THAT
FISHING TRIP.

Now arrange the circled letters to form the
surprise answer, as suggested by the above
cartoon.

Print answer here ⬡⬡⬡⬡ A ⬡⬡⬡⬡

JUMBLE®

Unscramble these four Jumbles, one letter to each square, to form four ordinary words.

LAWZT

PUPER

ENNKLE

YAWNAY

WHEN HE SAW THE COPS, THE ROBBER TOOK OFF AND LEFT HIS ACCOMPLICE TO DO THIS.

Now arrange the circled letters to form the surprise answer, as suggested by the above cartoon.

Print answer here ◯◯◯◯ THE "◯◯◯◯"

JUMBLE®

Unscramble these four Jumbles, one letter to each square, to form four ordinary words.

PALPY

LURBY

MYFAIL

GLUNJE

THE KANGAROO VISITED A SHRINK BECAUSE HE HAD BEEN FEELING THIS LATELY.

Now arrange the circled letters to form the surprise answer, as suggested by the above cartoon.

Print answer here

JUMBLE®

Unscramble these four Jumbles, one letter to each square, to form four ordinary words.

REBBI

KLANF

YOMFID

CINTAG

Saves me so much work

WHEN THEY INVENTED DRIP-DRY CLOTHES, THIS JUST ABOUT CAME TO AN END.

Now arrange the circled letters to form the surprise answer, as suggested by the above cartoon.

Print answer here THE ◯◯◯◯◯ ◯◯◯

JUMBLE®

Unscramble these four Jumbles, one letter to each square, to form four ordinary words.

PYKER

GWEED

RADACE

GREEME

HAIR SALON

Couldn't care less

PEOPLE WHO DON'T DYE THEIR HAIR COULD EVENTUALLY DO THIS.

Now arrange the circled letters to form the surprise answer, as suggested by the above cartoon.

Print answer here ⬡⬡⬡⬡ THE " ⬡⬡⬡⬡⬡⬡ "

JUMBLE®

Unscramble these four Jumbles, one letter to each square, to form four ordinary words.

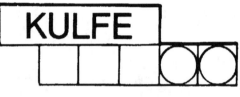

KULFE

COAME

AFAIRS

NOGARD

Hi, pal

FRANKENSTEIN WAS LONELY UNTIL HE DISCOVERED HOW TO DO THIS.

Now arrange the circled letters to form the surprise answer, as suggested by the above cartoon.

Print answer here

JUMBLE®

Unscramble these four Jumbles, one letter to
each square, to form four ordinary words.

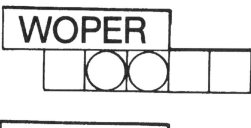

WOPER

TABOL

CLAFIA

VELCOR

WHAT HAPPENED
WHEN HE PUT
DYNAMITE INTO
THE REFRIGERATOR?

Now arrange the circled letters to form the
surprise answer, as suggested by the above
cartoon.

Print answer here HE ⬡⬡⬡⬡⬡ HIS ⬡⬡⬡⬡

JUMBLE®

Unscramble these four Jumbles, one letter to each square, to form four ordinary words.

PRAVO

TILEE

HARTOX

RICHEP

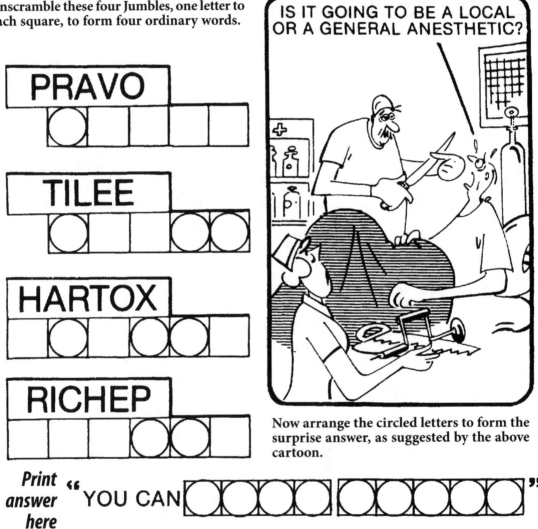

IS IT GOING TO BE A LOCAL OR A GENERAL ANESTHETIC?

Now arrange the circled letters to form the surprise answer, as suggested by the above cartoon.

Print answer here " YOU CAN ⬡⬡⬡⬡⬡ ⬡⬡⬡⬡⬡ "

JUMBLE®

Unscramble these four Jumbles, one letter to
each square, to form four ordinary words.

RUETT

CUEJI

DESSUR

JOADIN

WHAT THE LAWYER
DEMANDED TO HAVE
WITH HIS DRINK.

Now arrange the circled letters to form the
surprise answer, as suggested by the above
cartoon.

Print answer here "◯◯◯◯◯ ◯◯◯"

15

JUMBLE®

Unscramble these four Jumbles, one letter to
each square, to form four ordinary words.

RAYIF

NEEYM

RUPPEA

ALLTOW

WHAT THE RAM
SAID TO THE
FEMALE OF THE
SPECIES.

Now arrange the circled letters to form the
surprise answer, as suggested by the above
cartoon.

Print answer here ◯'◯ ◯◯◯◯◯ ◯◯◯

JUMBLE®

Unscramble these four Jumbles, one letter to each square, to form four ordinary words.

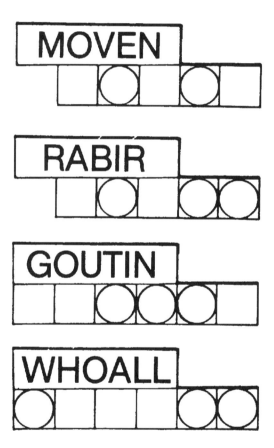

MOVEN

RABIR

GOUTIN

WHOALL

THE MINER DIDN'T KNOW WHETHER HE HAD STRUCK THIS.

Now arrange the circled letters to form the surprise answer, as suggested by the above cartoon.

Print answer here

17

JUMBLE®

Unscramble these four Jumbles, one letter to
each square, to form four ordinary words.

MEPOT

CUNEL

WOTOWK

THANYS

WHO'S HEARD ABOUT THE
BIG KIDNAPPING?

Now arrange the circled letters to form the
surprise answer, as suggested by the above
cartoon.

Print answer here " ◯◯ ◯◯◯◯◯ ◯◯ "

JUMBLE®

Unscramble these four Jumbles, one letter to
each square, to form four ordinary words.

CIRLY

BLYUL

FLORAM

PREFIL

HOW SHE SLIPPED
INTO HER BIKINI.

Now arrange the circled letters to form the
surprise answer, as suggested by the above
cartoon.

Print answer here "  "

JUMBLE®

Unscramble these four Jumbles, one letter to each square, to form four ordinary words.

MUHID

ANGLD

ERKLAT

PUCHIC

THE GOAT ATE AN ELECTRIC BULB BECAUSE ALL HE WANTED WAS THIS.

Now arrange the circled letters to form the surprise answer, as suggested by the above cartoon.

Print answer here A

JUMBLE®

Unscramble these four Jumbles, one letter to each square, to form four ordinary words.

NORST

ASAIL

LAISOR

SOXEEP

IT WAS HIS LAST MEAL, BUT YOU SHOULD HAVE SEEN THIS.

Now arrange the circled letters to form the surprise answer, as suggested by the above cartoon.

Print answer here HOW THE

21

JUMBLE®

Unscramble these four Jumbles, one letter to each square, to form four ordinary words.

CASEE

LARAT

ELLBOW

FEEDAC

THE CROOKED ARCHI-
TECT DISCOVERED THAT
PRISON WALLS WEREN'T
BUILT THIS WAY.

Now arrange the circled letters to form the surprise answer, as suggested by the above cartoon.

Print answer here

JUMBLE®

Unscramble these four Jumbles, one letter to each square, to form four ordinary words.

ORFOL

REFAT

LAYGEL

FELBAF

HE DECIDED TO RETIRE AFTER HIS PERFORMANCES BEGAN TO DO THIS.

Now arrange the circled letters to form the surprise answer, as suggested by the above cartoon.

Print answer here

JUMBLE®

Unscramble these four Jumbles, one letter to each square, to form four ordinary words.

WENIT

FITAH

PHISBO

PRAULL

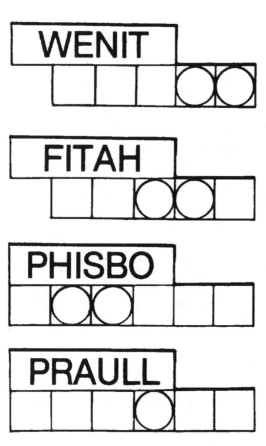

THE LIBRARIAN ALSO CRIED WHEN SHE SAW HER BOOKS WERE THIS.

Now arrange the circled letters to form the surprise answer, as suggested by the above cartoon.

Print answer here

JUMBLE

Unscramble these four Jumbles, one letter to each square, to form four ordinary words.

ENCAP

REVUC

MACIOT

RAHPON

LOANS

HE WAS SO BROKE THAT ALL THE PICK-POCKET GOT FROM HIM WAS THIS.

Now arrange the circled letters to form the surprise answer, as suggested by the above cartoon.

Print answer here

JUMBLE®

Unscramble these four Jumbles, one letter to each square, to form four ordinary words.

NIGGO

MONDE

CHYPIS

AFDACE

WHAT THAT MUTT
LIKED BEST
FOR BREAKFAST.

Now arrange the circled letters to form the surprise answer, as suggested by the above cartoon.

Print answer here "⬡⬡⬡⬡⬡⬡⬡⬡" ⬡⬡⬡⬡

JUMBLE Genius

Daily Puzzles

JUMBLE®

Unscramble these four Jumbles, one letter to each square, to form four ordinary words.

HOBAR

ALGOT

SCOTUC

HYSERR

What do you do with the middle part?

EASY FOR A RE-
PORTER TO GET
AT A DOUGHNUT
SHOP.

Now arrange the circled letters to form the surprise answer, as suggested by the above cartoon.

Print answer here THE " ⟨◯◯◯◯◯⟩ " ⟨◯◯◯◯◯◯⟩

JUMBLE®

Unscramble these four Jumbles, one letter to each square, to form four ordinary words.

REELD

SERCS

FREPER

LEXFAN

I'm fine

HOW SHE FELT WHEN THE DOCTOR SAID, "NO PROB-LEM, NO CHARGE".

Now arrange the circled letters to form the surprise answer, as suggested by the above cartoon.

Print answer here ◯◯◯◯ " ◯◯◯◯ "

JUMBLE®

Unscramble these four Jumbles, one letter to
each square, to form four ordinary words.

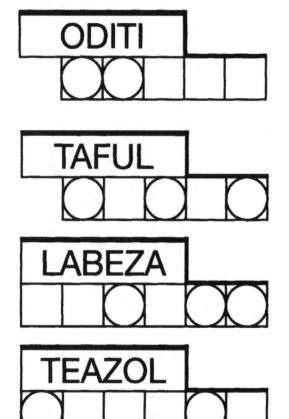

ODITI

TAFUL

LABEZA

TEAZOL

I give up

THIS HAPPENED
WHEN HE TRIED
TO DRINK A
CASE OF SODA.

Now arrange the circled letters to form the
surprise answer, as suggested by the above
cartoon.

Print answer here **HE** " ◯◯◯◯◯◯◯◯ " ◯◯◯

JUMBLE®

Unscramble these four Jumbles, one letter to each square, to form four ordinary words.

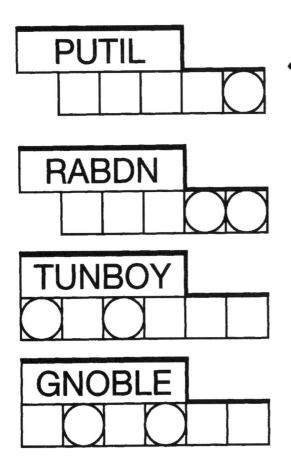

PUTIL

RABDN

TUNBOY

GNOBLE

HOW THE SHOW DOG PREPARED FOR THE COMPETITION.

Now arrange the circled letters to form the surprise answer, as suggested by the above cartoon.

Print answer here HE

JUMBLE®

Unscramble these four Jumbles, one letter to each square, to form four ordinary words.

SUGES

SASEY

DRAISH

PRAULL

He sure loves his work

HOW THE HOT DOG VENDOR TACKLED HIS JOB.

Now arrange the circled letters to form the surprise answer, as suggested by the above cartoon.

Print answer here   **WITH** " ◯◯◯◯◯◯ "

JUMBLE®

Unscramble these four Jumbles, one letter to each square, to form four ordinary words.

NELIR

GURPE

NOTAIR

BAHCLE

Qualified employees are essential

JOB RECRUITMENT

WHY THE COMPANY'S PRESIDENT WENT BACK TO SCHOOL.

Now arrange the circled letters to form the surprise answer, as suggested by the above cartoon.

Print answer here FOR "〇〇〇〇" 〇〇〇〇〇〇〇〇

JUMBLE®

Unscramble these four Jumbles, one letter to each square, to form four ordinary words.

VASUE

RAMOJ

DYRAHL

DINCAR

Five days till vacation

We're going on a cruise

Xmas clearance

WHAT THE DE-PARTMENT STORE CLERKS LOOKED FORWARD TO.

Now arrange the circled letters to form the surprise answer, as suggested by the above cartoon.

Print answer here **A**

JUMBLE®

Unscramble these four Jumbles, one letter to each square, to form four ordinary words.

OPTIA

THABI

YARRIT

SOXEEP

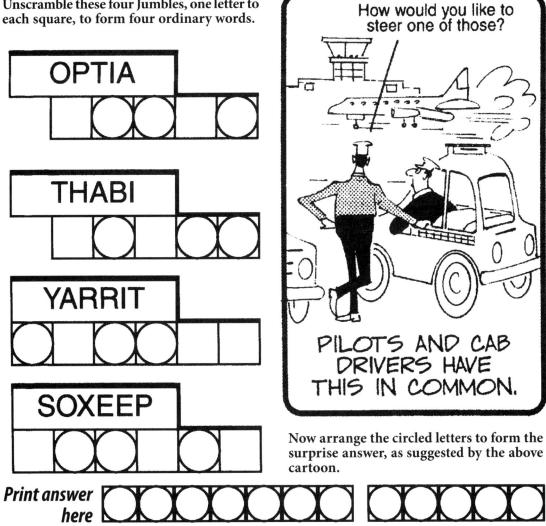

How would you like to steer one of those?

PILOTS AND CAB DRIVERS HAVE THIS IN COMMON.

Now arrange the circled letters to form the surprise answer, as suggested by the above cartoon.

Print answer here

JUMBLE®

Unscramble these four Jumbles, one letter to
each square, to form four ordinary words.

TOFLY

GOBUM

YIRAWA

FLUIFT

75 in 40
mile zone

Where did you
hatch those
numbers?

WHAT HAPPENED
WHEN THE ROOSTER
WAS STOPPED
FOR SPEEDING.

Now arrange the circled letters to form the
surprise answer, as suggested by the above
cartoon.

*Print
answer* **THE** ⭕⭕⭕⭕ **RAN** ⭕⭕⭕⭕⭕
here

JUMBLE®

Unscramble these four Jumbles, one letter to
each square, to form four ordinary words.

KEREC

HYLYS

MOAWED

LAWASY

Everyone's having fun but me

HOW MOM FELT WHILE SHE DARNED SOCKS.

Now arrange the circled letters to form the
surprise answer, as suggested by the above
cartoon.

Print answer here ◯◯◯ - ◯◯◯

JUMBLE®

Unscramble these four Jumbles, one letter to
each square, to form four ordinary words.

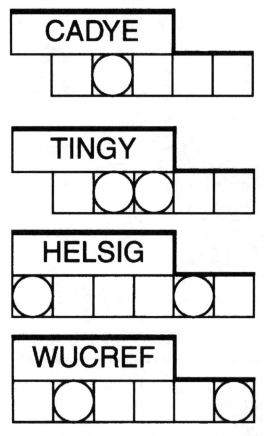

CADYE

TINGY

HELSIG

WUCREF

Leave him alone, he helps
me with tests

WHAT THE
STREET THUGS
CONSIDERED
THE WHIZ KID.

Now arrange the circled letters to form the
surprise answer, as suggested by the above
cartoon.

Print answer here **A** "  "

JUMBLE®

Unscramble these four Jumbles, one letter to each square, to form four ordinary words.

IDLAY

LEREC

CAPMEN

VOCONY

EL SWANKO

Welcome, Miss La Sauche

It's the spot to be seen

WHY EVERYONE WANTED TO STAY AT THE POPULAR HOTEL.

Now arrange the circled letters to form the surprise answer, as suggested by the above cartoon.

Print answer here IT **WAS THE** " ⟡⟡⟡ " ⟡⟡⟡⟡⟡

JUMBLE®

Unscramble these four Jumbles, one letter to
each square, to form four ordinary words.

TRAIE

ZIPER

BARTUN

CINTAG

This is
how he
relaxes

WHAT THE GLOBAL
STRATEGIST
FOCUSED ON
DURING HIS
LEISURE TIME.

Now arrange the circled letters to form the
surprise answer, as suggested by the above
cartoon.

*Print
answer* **THE** ⬡⬡⬡ ⬡⬡⬡⬡⬡⬡⬡
here

JUMBLE®

Unscramble these four Jumbles, one letter to each square, to form four ordinary words.

ENCEF

VEGIN

FELGUN

VIRQUE

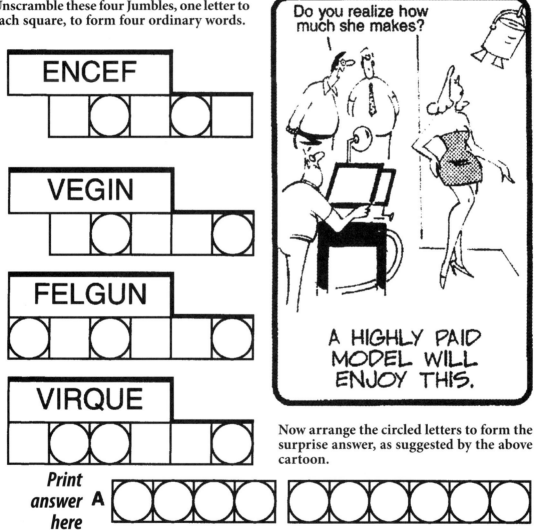

Do you realize how much she makes?

A HIGHLY PAID MODEL WILL ENJOY THIS.

Now arrange the circled letters to form the surprise answer, as suggested by the above cartoon.

Print answer here **A**

JUMBLE®

Unscramble these four Jumbles, one letter to
each square, to form four ordinary words.

TUMON

GLITH

MIRVEN

RIJEGG

Watch how fast I
can do this, Pop

WHY THE OLD
TIMER ENVIED
THE YOUNG
MECHANIC.

Now arrange the circled letters to form the
surprise answer, as suggested by the above
cartoon.

Print answer HE "◯◯-◯◯◯◯◯◯◯"
here WAS

JUMBLE®

Unscramble these four Jumbles, one letter to each square, to form four ordinary words.

TEFAC

ROGUD

GRAVEA

CHOROB

He has great concentration

NEEDED TO BE A GOOD SOCCER PLAYER.

Now arrange the circled letters to form the surprise answer, as suggested by the above cartoon.

Print answer here A ⬭⬭⬭⬭ ⬭⬭⬭ IT

JUMBLE®

Unscramble these four Jumbles, one letter to each square, to form four ordinary words.

TAGUM

YURMM

TRUXAS

HUNGOE

I told you to fill up earlier

WHAT BACKSEAT DRIVERS NEVER DO.

Now arrange the circled letters to form the surprise answer, as suggested by the above cartoon.

Print answer here

☐☐☐ ☐☐☐ OF " ☐☐☐ "

JUMBLE®

Unscramble these four Jumbles, one letter to each square, to form four ordinary words.

TINJO

BOMIL

TYNTOK

GRANAH

...and $100 to George for his money-saving plan

A GOOD IDEA CAN LEAD TO THIS.

Now arrange the circled letters to form the surprise answer, as suggested by the above cartoon.

Print answer here ⬡⬡⬡⬡⬡ **OF A** ⬡⬡⬡⬡⬡⬡

JUMBLE®

Unscramble these four Jumbles, one letter to each square, to form four ordinary words.

DUGAY

YEVAH

GUEMLE

FRIPOT

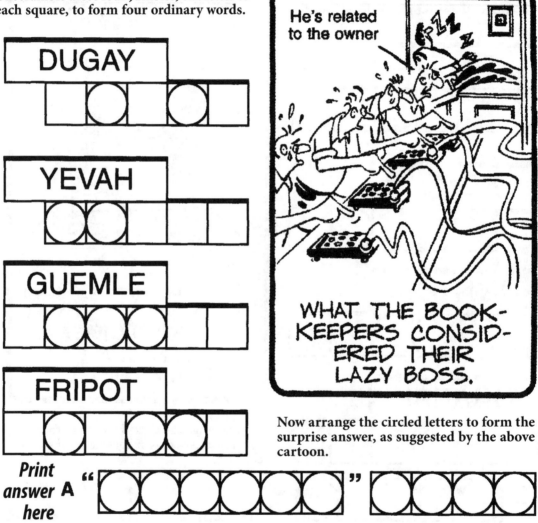

He's related to the owner

WHAT THE BOOK-KEEPERS CONSID-ERED THEIR LAZY BOSS.

Now arrange the circled letters to form the surprise answer, as suggested by the above cartoon.

Print answer A " ⬡⬡⬡⬡⬡⬡ " ⬡⬡⬡⬡
here

JUMBLE®

Unscramble these four Jumbles, one letter to each square, to form four ordinary words.

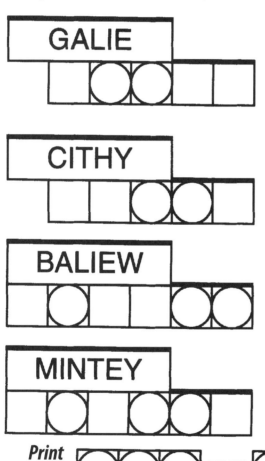

GALIE

CITHY

BALIEW

MINTEY

I just finished cleaning it

MOM CAN DO THIS OVER A DIRTY FLOOR.

Now arrange the circled letters to form the surprise answer, as suggested by the above cartoon.

Print answer here ⬡⬡⬡ **THE** ⬡⬡⬡⬡⬡⬡⬡

JUMBLE®

Unscramble these four Jumbles, one letter to
each square, to form four ordinary words.

IRYAH

WOLLY

MUBIDE

NAUMUT

You're giving me
a headache

WHAT THE BABY
SITTER HAD
WHEN THE INFANT
GOT CRABBY.

Now arrange the circled letters to form the
surprise answer, as suggested by the above
cartoon.

Print answer
here   A "☐☐☐☐" OF
            A ☐☐☐☐

JUMBLE®

Unscramble these four Jumbles, one letter to
each square, to form four ordinary words.

HEMTY

TOIDI

RAMIED

LAKLIA

HOW THE DRIVER
WANTED HIS RACE
CAR TO PERFORM.

Now arrange the circled letters to form the
surprise answer, as suggested by the above
cartoon.

Print answer here ⬚⬚⬚⬚ A ⬚⬚⬚⬚⬚

JUMBLE®

Unscramble these four Jumbles, one letter to each square, to form four ordinary words.

CAINB

GOBTE

NARTOM

LAUTES

I've got to get an accountant

WHAT THE COFFEE PLANTATION OWNER NEEDED.

Now arrange the circled letters to form the surprise answer, as suggested by the above cartoon.

Print answer **A** here

JUMBLE®

Unscramble these four Jumbles, one letter to each square, to form four ordinary words.

YICIL

EPTIN

ILCAME

ENERGE

Worse than ever

Such service!

HOW A LATE TRAIN ON A COLD MORNING LEFT THE COMMUTERS.

Now arrange the circled letters to form the surprise answer, as suggested by the above cartoon.

Print answer here

JUMBLE®

Unscramble these four Jumbles, one letter to each square, to form four ordinary words.

RACCK

VELOR

SHORCC

HARTHS

Yuck – I'm outta here

WHAT THE ACTOR-TURNED-FISHERMAN GOT FROM HIS DATE.

Now arrange the circled letters to form the surprise answer, as suggested by the above cartoon.

Print answer here

JUMBLE®

Unscramble these four Jumbles, one letter to each square, to form four ordinary words.

DARNB

BECAL

FASTIE

ATVARC

I've ruined our getaway

GETTING SICK AT A RUSTIC HIDE-AWAY CAN LEAVE YOU WITH ---

Now arrange the circled letters to form the surprise answer, as suggested by the above cartoon.

Print answer here

" "

JUMBLE®

Unscramble these four Jumbles, one letter to each square, to form four ordinary words.

CUROC

WHAAS

TERRFE

TANNIF

Such sweeping strokes

It takes great control

POSSESSED BY A CALLIGRAPHER.

Now arrange the circled letters to form the surprise answer, as suggested by the above cartoon.

Print answer here   THE ☐☐☐☐☐☐   ☐☐☐☐☐☐

JUMBLE®

Unscramble these four Jumbles, one letter to each square, to form four ordinary words.

WOGAL

GANOW

TECTAL

ULSSET

Ouch!   Just follow my lead

WHAT IT TAKES
TO ARGUE OVER
A DANCE STEP.

Now arrange the circled letters to form the surprise answer, as suggested by the above cartoon.

Print answer here ◯◯◯ **TO** ◯◯◯◯◯◯

JUMBLE®

Unscramble these four Jumbles, one letter to each square, to form four ordinary words.

BOVAR

ERBLE

DAPOAG

GILBOE

Won't be in today, sore throat

USEFUL WHEN SNEAKING OUT FOR A ROUND OF GOLF.

Now arrange the circled letters to form the surprise answer, as suggested by the above cartoon.

Print answer here **A** ⬡⬡⬡⬡ ⬡⬡⬡

JUMBLE®

Unscramble these four Jumbles, one letter to each square, to form four ordinary words.

NEFEC

OSPOT

SURIAD

CAFEDE

You look terrific

A STRICT DIET GAVE HIM THIS.

Now arrange the circled letters to form the surprise answer, as suggested by the above cartoon.

Print answer here

JUMBLE®

Unscramble these four Jumbles, one letter to each square, to form four ordinary words.

TALGO

TIDEF

VISNAH

GAMANE

These feel good. I'll take them

At last

WHAT THE FUSSY CUSTOMER FINALLY DID TO THE SALESMAN.

Now arrange the circled letters to form the surprise answer, as suggested by the above cartoon.

Print answer here

A

JUMBLE®

Unscramble these four Jumbles, one letter to
each square, to form four ordinary words.

SYSAG

PRUPE

HUMBAS

THUGOR

Sorry, I can
hardly talk

Ahchoo!

HOW THE HANSOM
DRIVER ENDED UP
WHEN HE CAUGHT
A COLD.

Now arrange the circled letters to form the
surprise answer, as suggested by the above
cartoon.

**Print
answer
here** ⭕⭕⭕⭕⭕⭕ **AND** ⭕⭕⭕⭕⭕

JUMBLE®

Unscramble these four Jumbles, one letter to each square, to form four ordinary words.

ACOOC

LEXEP

NUTTAR

MEEZAC

Let me introduce our new president

I remember when he had hair

HOW THE BALDING MANAGER FARED IN THE RACE FOR THE JOB.

Now arrange the circled letters to form the surprise answer, as suggested by the above cartoon.

Print answer here HE ⬡⬡⬡⬡ ⬡⬡⬡ ON ⬡⬡⬡

JUMBLE®

Unscramble these four Jumbles, one letter to each square, to form four ordinary words.

SAYES

EXOID

DOUBIT

NURUTE

WHAT THE MUSIC STUDENT DID BEFORE THE TEST.

Now arrange the circled letters to form the surprise answer, as suggested by the above cartoon.

Print answer here ⬡⬡⬡⬡⬡⬡⬡ HIS " ⬡⬡⬡⬡⬡ "

JUMBLE®

Unscramble these four Jumbles, one letter to each square, to form four ordinary words.

GLIYN

LUFAW

AUVEEN

DROINO

HOW MOM ENDED UP WHEN JUNIOR GOT INTO THE SEWING BOX.

Now arrange the circled letters to form the surprise answer, as suggested by the above cartoon.

Print answer here

JUMBLE®

Unscramble these four Jumbles, one letter to
each square, to form four ordinary words.

NYKAL

TUDAL

TELTEK

BUBYCH

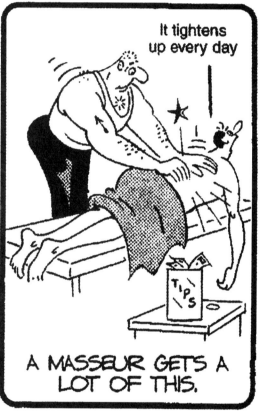

It tightens
up every day

A MASSEUR GETS A
LOT OF THIS.

Now arrange the circled letters to form the
surprise answer, as suggested by the above
cartoon.

Print answer here

JUMBLE®

Unscramble these four Jumbles, one letter to
each square, to form four ordinary words.

MORRA

SULOE

FALLUW

MIDYOF

Do you have
an explanation?

WHAT HE SAID TO
DAD WHEN HE
FLUNKED THE
SPELLING TEST.

Now arrange the circled letters to form the
surprise answer, as suggested by the above
cartoon.

Print
answer
here "   "

JUMBLE®

Unscramble these four Jumbles, one letter to each square, to form four ordinary words.

DAAMM

IMMAX

PEESLY

PLESIV

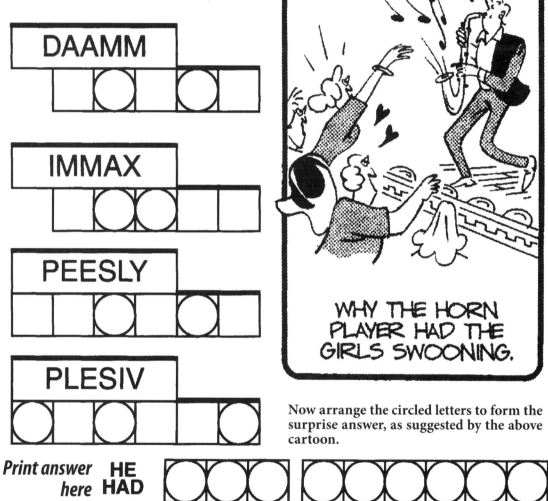

WHY THE HORN
PLAYER HAD THE
GIRLS SWOONING.

Now arrange the circled letters to form the surprise answer, as suggested by the above cartoon.

Print answer here **HE HAD**

JUMBLE®

Unscramble these four Jumbles, one letter to each square, to form four ordinary words.

DRUFA

AYLIG

YAWTER

DHELVA

I'll set it tonight

WHAT THEY ENDED UP WITH WHEN THEY DOVE INTO THE BREAKERS.

Now arrange the circled letters to form the surprise answer, as suggested by the above cartoon.

Print answer here " ◯◯◯◯ " ◯◯◯◯

JUMBLE

Unscramble these four Jumbles, one letter to each square, to form four ordinary words.

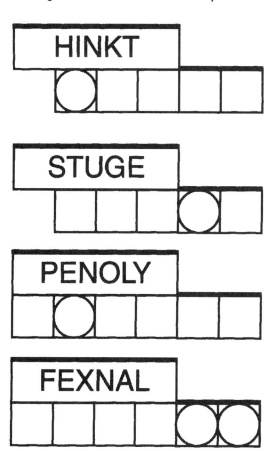

HINKT

STUGE

PENOLY

FEXNAL

I'm beat

And broke

HOW MOM FELT AFTER HER ALL-DAY SHOPPING SPREE.

Now arrange the circled letters to form the surprise answer, as suggested by the above cartoon.

Print answer here

JUMBLE®

Unscramble these four Jumbles, one letter to
each square, to form four ordinary words.

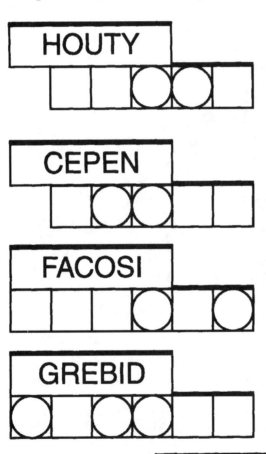

HOUTY

CEPEN

FACOSI

GREBID

The braces will
improve your smile

WHAT THE DENTIST
GAVE THE TV
REPORTER.

Now arrange the circled letters to form the
surprise answer, as suggested by the above
cartoon.

Print answer here **A** ◯◯◯◯◯ ◯◯◯◯

JUMBLE®

Unscramble these four Jumbles, one letter to each square, to form four ordinary words.

TRINP

HEMRY

SELAWE

REFOLG

Whew, 3 miles in 30 minutes

RUNNING ON A TREADMILL WILL GET YOU HERE.

Now arrange the circled letters to form the surprise answer, as suggested by the above cartoon.

Print answer here

JUMBLE®

Unscramble these four Jumbles, one letter to
each square, to form four ordinary words.

DRATY

LONBE

BITTID

REBALZ

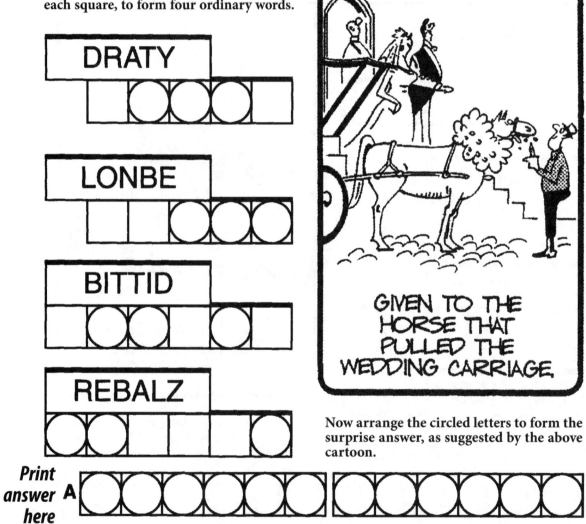

GIVEN TO THE
HORSE THAT
PULLED THE
WEDDING CARRIAGE.

Now arrange the circled letters to form the
surprise answer, as suggested by the above
cartoon.

Print
answer A
here

JUMBLE

Unscramble these four Jumbles, one letter to
each square, to form four ordinary words.

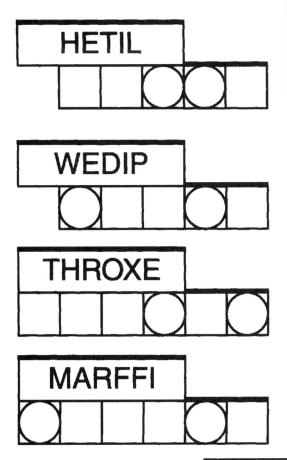

HETIL

WEDIP

THROXE

MARFFI

Both of you in the
tub right now!

WHERE THE KIDS
LANDED FOR
PLAYING IN THE MUD.

Now arrange the circled letters to form the
surprise answer, as suggested by the above
cartoon.

Print answer here **IN**

JUMBLE®

Unscramble these four Jumbles, one letter to
each square, to form four ordinary words.

TYKIT

KLANE

SEJERY

BLOWEB

They make
sure it's
right

WHY A BUILDING
SITE IS CAREFULLY
MEASURED.

Now arrange the circled letters to form the
surprise answer, as suggested by the above
cartoon.

Print
answer A " ☐☐☐ " IS AT ☐☐☐☐☐
here

JUMBLE®

Unscramble these four Jumbles, one letter to each square, to form four ordinary words.

MORIN

SYNAP

BIMGAT

GREATY

It's just not me

That's the ninth one she's had on

SHOPPING FOR A NEW OUTFIT USU-ALLY RESULTS IN THIS.

Now arrange the circled letters to form the surprise answer, as suggested by the above cartoon.

Print answer here " ◯◯◯◯◯◯ " ◯◯◯◯◯

JUMBLE®

Unscramble these four Jumbles, one letter to
each square, to form four ordinary words.

TEQUS

ESSOU

ENSTEW

SUCCAU

Magnificent

Worth every
penny

$$$

WHAT THE YOUNG
CHEF EXPERIENCED
WHEN HIS DISH
BECAME POPULAR.

Now arrange the circled letters to form the
surprise answer, as suggested by the above
cartoon.

Print
answer A " ⬡⬡⬡⬡⬡ " OF ⬡⬡⬡⬡⬡⬡⬡⬡
here

JUMBLE®

Unscramble these four Jumbles, one letter to each square, to form four ordinary words.

ORRUJ

HEMIC

BEMMER

DOWHAS

You are here

How far to ...?

ANOTHER NAME FOR A TOURIST INFOR-MATION CENTER.

Now arrange the circled letters to form the surprise answer, as suggested by the above cartoon.

Print answer here A " ☐☐☐☐☐ " ☐☐☐☐☐

JUMBLE®

Unscramble these four Jumbles, one letter to each square, to form four ordinary words.

GLARN

YEGEL

LASTOP

UNBOCE

I have the finest vintages money can buy

THE AUTHOR SAID HIS WINE COLLEC- TION WAS —

Now arrange the circled letters to form the surprise answer, as suggested by the above cartoon.

Print answer here **A** " ◯◯◯◯◯ ◯◯◯◯◯◯ "

JUMBLE®

Unscramble these four Jumbles, one letter to each square, to form four ordinary words.

ESROU

VERIP

IMVOTE

STEPEL

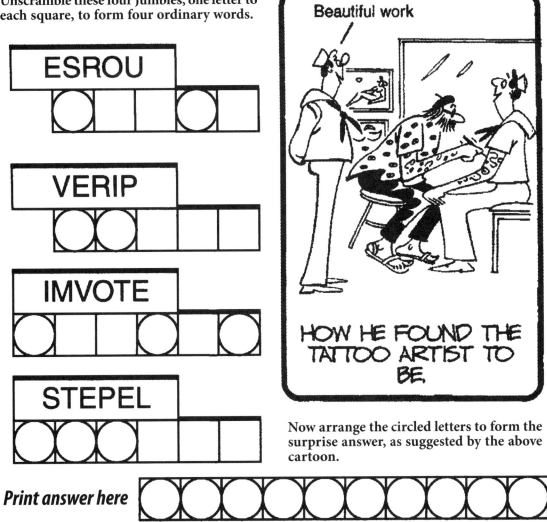

Beautiful work

HOW HE FOUND THE TATTOO ARTIST TO BE.

Now arrange the circled letters to form the surprise answer, as suggested by the above cartoon.

Print answer here

JUMBLE®

Unscramble these four Jumbles, one letter to each square, to form four ordinary words.

HOPAC

ORNOH

TRIMOP

YERSEG

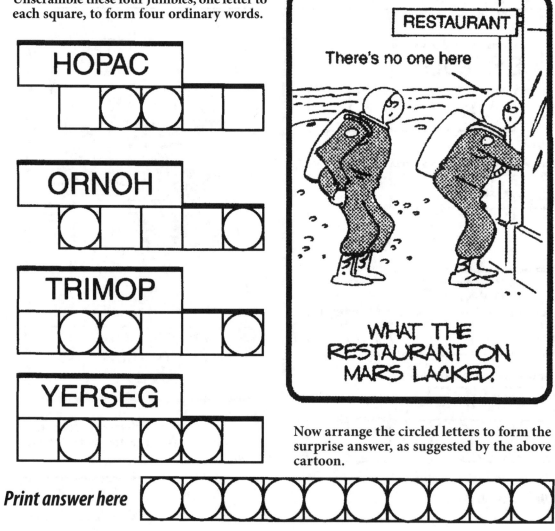

RESTAURANT

There's no one here

WHAT THE RESTAURANT ON MARS LACKED.

Now arrange the circled letters to form the surprise answer, as suggested by the above cartoon.

Print answer here

JUMBLE®

Unscramble these four Jumbles, one letter to each square, to form four ordinary words.

DEWUN

MOPET

CLOTUC

PHARIS

Just a little off the top

WHAT THE BARBER GAVE THE SAILORS.

Now arrange the circled letters to form the surprise answer, as suggested by the above cartoon.

Print answer here "◯◯◯◯" ◯◯◯◯

JUMBLE®

Unscramble these four Jumbles, one letter to each square, to form four ordinary words.

CANYF

INBOR

MORRAY

RAVEEB

You're 3 months behind

Calm down

THIS CAN OCCUR WHEN THE ALIMONY IS LATE.

Now arrange the circled letters to form the surprise answer, as suggested by the above cartoon.

Print answer here

JUMBLE®

Unscramble these four Jumbles, one letter to each square, to form four ordinary words.

VUCER

GIRRO

FORTYS

BURNEM

It's all ready for you, sir

FOUND AT MOST HOTELS.

Now arrange the circled letters to form the surprise answer, as suggested by the above cartoon.

Print answer here

JUMBLE®

Unscramble these four Jumbles, one letter to each square, to form four ordinary words.

GUPER

ASTUE

CEETIN

THINEZ

My work is always the best

WHAT THE SELF-CENTERED OPTOMETRIST GAVE HIS PATIENT.

Now arrange the circled letters to form the surprise answer, as suggested by the above cartoon.

Print answer here " ◯ " ◯◯◯◯◯◯

JUMBLE®

Unscramble these four Jumbles, one letter to each square, to form four ordinary words.

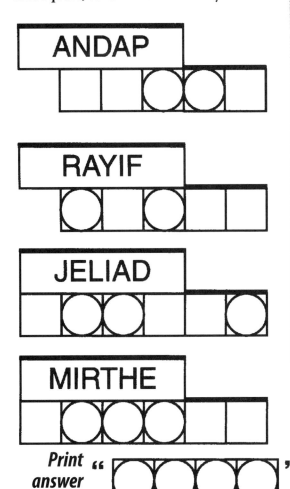

ANDAP

RAYIF

JELIAD

MIRTHE

Good work, you deserve a raise

WHAT A CARNIVAL BOSS MUST ALWAYS BE.

Now arrange the circled letters to form the surprise answer, as suggested by the above cartoon.

Print answer here "⟨◯◯◯◯⟩" ⟨◯◯◯◯◯◯◯⟩

JUMBLE®

Unscramble these four Jumbles, one letter to each square, to form four ordinary words.

LIPTO

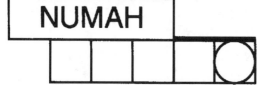

NUMAH

SAVILE

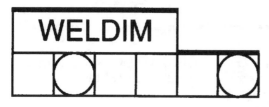

WELDIM

Oops!   #$%&!!

WHERE THE CLUMSY HELPER LEFT THE CHEF.

Now arrange the circled letters to form the surprise answer, as suggested by the above cartoon.

Print answer here A

JUMBLE®

Unscramble these four Jumbles, one letter to
each square, to form four ordinary words.

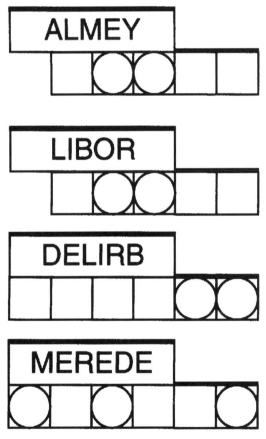

ALMEY

LIBOR

DELIRB

MEREDE

Here's one for
a dozen ties

THE KIND OF
BUSINESS THE
CATALOG HOUSE
GOT FROM MEN.

Now arrange the circled letters to form the
surprise answer, as suggested by the above
cartoon.

Print answer here " ◯◯◯◯ " ◯◯◯◯◯◯

JUMBLE®

Unscramble these four Jumbles, one letter to
each square, to form four ordinary words.

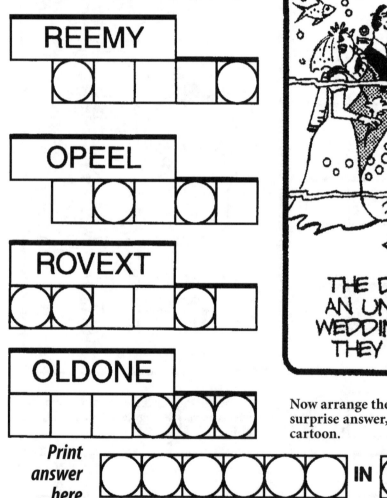

REEMY

OPEEL

ROVEXT

OLDONE

Do you take this woman ...

THE DIVERS HAD
AN UNDERWATER
WEDDING BECAUSE
THEY WERE ——

Now arrange the circled letters to form the
surprise answer, as suggested by the above
cartoon.

*Print
answer
here*

◯◯◯◯◯◯ IN ◯◯◯◯

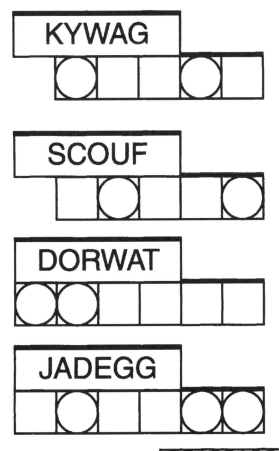

JUMBLE®

Unscramble these four Jumbles, one letter to each square, to form four ordinary words.

KYWAG

SCOUF

DORWAT

JADEGG

That'll be fifty bucks

THIS HAPPENED WHEN HE BOUGHT AN UMBRELLA IN THE RAIN.

Now arrange the circled letters to form the surprise answer, as suggested by the above cartoon.

Print answer here **HE** ◯◯◯ ◯◯◯◯◯◯

JUMBLE.

Unscramble these four Jumbles, one letter to
each square, to form four ordinary words.

MYOFA

CLIVI

BENEAT

PAPNYS

That's not me

I'll soften the nose and eyes

WHY HE ALTERED HER PORTRAIT.

Now arrange the circled letters to form the
surprise answer, as suggested by the above
cartoon.

Print answer here **TO**

JUMBLE®

Unscramble these four Jumbles, one letter to
each square, to form four ordinary words.

YETTS

VOLGE

DAYDEL

RIVUTE

Perfect —

USED TO MAKE
WEDDING VEILS.

Now arrange the circled letters to form the
surprise answer, as suggested by the above
cartoon.

**Print
answer
here**

OF
THE

JUMBLE®

Unscramble these four Jumbles, one letter to
each square, to form four ordinary words.

YEMSS

DERIN

ONGARD

TRINWY

I'm ready

That's awful, go change right now!

WHAT HE GOT
FROM MOM FOR
NOT DRESSING UP.

Now arrange the circled letters to form the
surprise answer, as suggested by the above
cartoon.

Print answer here **A**

JUMBLE®

Unscramble these four Jumbles, one letter to each square, to form four ordinary words.

CIMER

MESOO

TURBLE

ENBRAY

I'm losing weight, but this is expensive

The fewer the calories, the more you pay

A NO-FAT DIET ON A TIGHT BUDGET CAN LEAD TO THIS.

Now arrange the circled letters to form the surprise answer, as suggested by the above cartoon.

Print answer here

JUMBLE®

Unscramble these four Jumbles, one letter to each square, to form four ordinary words.

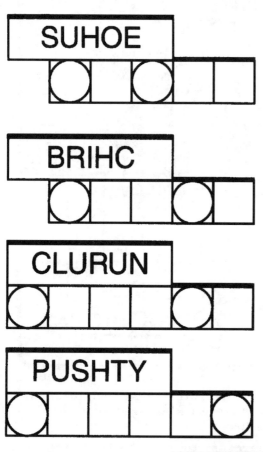

SUHOE

BRIHC

CLURUN

PUSHTY

It'll keep you cool in summer

WHAT THE BARBER GAVE THE ARTIST.

Now arrange the circled letters to form the surprise answer, as suggested by the above cartoon.

Print answer here A "  "

JUMBLE®

Unscramble these four Jumbles, one letter to each square, to form four ordinary words.

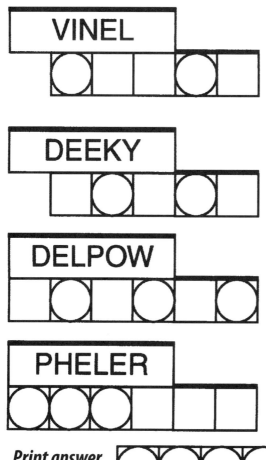

VINEL

DEEKY

DELPOW

PHELER

Feel like new, and I saved $100

HOW HE FELT WHEN HIS SHOES WERE REPAIRED.

Now arrange the circled letters to form the surprise answer, as suggested by the above cartoon.

Print answer here

JUMBLE®

Unscramble these four Jumbles, one letter to each square, to form four ordinary words.

PLIME

VOLEN

HIRSLE

SLIMIE

You have just won ...

... Just five easy payments

USEFUL TOOLS FOR SOME SOLICITORS.

Now arrange the circled letters to form the surprise answer, as suggested by the above cartoon.

Print " ⎡◯◯◯◯⎤ " ⎡◯◯◯◯◯◯⎤
answer
here

JUMBLE®

Unscramble these four Jumbles, one letter to each square, to form four ordinary words.

IXOCT

UPYPP

NOYRAC

WROFUR

WHERE HE STOOD ON HELPING WITH THE HOUSEWORK.

Now arrange the circled letters to form the surprise answer, as suggested by the above cartoon.

Print answer here ⭘⭘⭘ **OF THE** ⭘⭘⭘

JUMBLE®

Unscramble these four Jumbles, one letter to each square, to form four ordinary words.

BROIT

DORBO

CYSTOL

PARTIE

I won't be long. Make sure he eats his peas

ANOTHER NAME FOR A HIGH CHAIR.

Now arrange the circled letters to form the surprise answer, as suggested by the above cartoon.

Print answer here **A**

JUMBLE®

Unscramble these four Jumbles, one letter to each square, to form four ordinary words.

FUINY

LOFUR

CROGED

TYDWAR

Mom, I need these tomorrow

HOW MOM FELT AFTER DOING LAUNDRY ALL DAY.

Now arrange the circled letters to form the surprise answer, as suggested by the above cartoon.

Print answer here

JUMBLE®

Unscramble these four Jumbles, one letter to
each square, to form four ordinary words.

UPASE

IRATT

HUPNAC

MENECT

Strange creatures, aren't they?

WHAT THE COWS
WATCHED DURING
THE MARATHON.

Now arrange the circled letters to form the
surprise answer, as suggested by the above
cartoon.

Print answer here **THE**

JUMBLE®

Unscramble these four Jumbles, one letter to each square, to form four ordinary words.

POVER

SHUBY

LAWSUR

WOFELL

You're getting there. Keep practicing

HOW THE NEEDLE-POINT INSTRUCTOR DESCRIBED HER WORK.

Now arrange the circled letters to form the surprise answer, as suggested by the above cartoon.

Print answer here ◯◯◯◯-◯◯◯

JUMBLE.

Unscramble these four Jumbles, one letter to each square, to form four ordinary words.

SYNOW

COEMA

SUDJAT

SOUNIC

YOU MIGHT CALL MAKING PRESERVES THIS.

Now arrange the circled letters to form the surprise answer, as suggested by the above cartoon.

Print answer here A ⬚⬚⬚ ⬚⬚⬚⬚⬚⬚⬚

JUMBLE®

Unscramble these four Jumbles, one letter to
each square, to form four ordinary words.

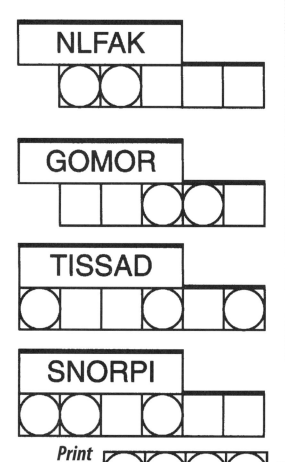

NLFAK

GOMOR

TISSAD

SNORPI

It stops the sniffles
in 24 hours

... and maybe
the red ink

WHAT THE
COMPANY HOPED
ITS NEW DRUG
WOULD CURE.

Now arrange the circled letters to form the
surprise answer, as suggested by the above
cartoon.

*Print
answer
here*

OF

JUMBLE®

Unscramble these four Jumbles, one letter to
each square, to form four ordinary words.

ALQUI

YANER

WERDOP

ERPICH

Can you put a ribbon around it?

IMPORTANT FOR A GIFT OF HIP-HOP MUSIC.

Now arrange the circled letters to form the
surprise answer, as suggested by the above
cartoon.

Print answer here **A** ◯◯◯ ◯◯◯◯

JUMBLE®

Unscramble these four Jumbles, one letter to each square, to form four ordinary words.

SQUAH

RAWEY

LEMDEY

BLUMFE

Doesn't anyone turn off the lights?!

WHAT DAD DID WHEN HE GOT THE ELECTRIC BILL

Now arrange the circled letters to form the surprise answer, as suggested by the above cartoon.

Print answer here A

JUMBLE®

Unscramble these four Jumbles, one letter to
each square, to form four ordinary words.

BYLUR

SARVO

KHEELS

YINJET

WHAT THE INEPT
CARPENTER'S
HELPER TRIED TO
DO.

Now arrange the circled letters to form the
surprise answer, as suggested by the above
cartoon.

Print
answer **HIS** " ⃝⃝⃝⃝⃝ " ⃝⃝⃝⃝
here

JUMBLE®

Unscramble these four Jumbles, one letter to
each square, to form four ordinary words.

TYIDE

GINES

TURGED

CIRNUH

I told you to
quit an hour ago

THIS CAN HAPPEN
WHEN A CRAPS
SHOOTER LOSES.

Now arrange the circled letters to form the
surprise answer, as suggested by the above
cartoon.

*Print
answer
here*

GET

JUMBLE®

Unscramble these four Jumbles, one letter to each square, to form four ordinary words.

THOOP

ROBOK

GUNJEL

FATOLA

TOUGH TO DO
WHEN SUFFERING
FROM LARYNGITIS.

Now arrange the circled letters to form the surprise answer, as suggested by the above cartoon.

Print
answer
here

IT

JUMBLE

Unscramble these four Jumbles, one letter to each square, to form four ordinary words.

YIZZD

CROFE

LOYDOG

SHRAIG

I can't believe we're back

I can't remember a thing

WHAT STUDENTS EXPERIENCE AFTER A LONG SUMMER BREAK.

Now arrange the circled letters to form the surprise answer, as suggested by the above cartoon.

Print answer here

JUMBLE®

Unscramble these four Jumbles, one letter to each square, to form four ordinary words.

VOYIR

PODEK

SNORGT

FRINIM

I'm going in   They're eating me up

SNORKELERS AND MOSQUITOES HAVE THIS IN COMMON.

Now arrange the circled letters to form the surprise answer, as suggested by the above cartoon.

Print answer here

JUMBLE®

Unscramble these four Jumbles, one letter to each square, to form four ordinary words.

TEMPY

FIDOR

BONYED

RENOCE

This used to be so easy

Where're your glasses?

WHAT YOU NEED TO THREAD A NEEDLE.

Now arrange the circled letters to form the surprise answer, as suggested by the above cartoon.

Print answer here AN ⬡⬡⬡ ⬡⬡⬡ ⬡⬡

JUMBLE®

Unscramble these four Jumbles, one letter to each square, to form four ordinary words.

YURUS

KLIMY

PECTOK

INBELB

I thought you quit

That was last week

WHERE HIS RESOLUTION TO STOP USING CIGARETTES WENT.

Now arrange the circled letters to form the surprise answer, as suggested by the above cartoon.

Print answer here

JUMBLE®

Unscramble these four Jumbles, one letter to
each square, to form four ordinary words.

SAYTH

RAWFE

MUCAUV

DRAFTI

Slow down!

HIS FIRST SHIFT
AT THE SAUSAGE
FACTORY TURNED
INTO THIS.

Now arrange the circled letters to form the
surprise answer, as suggested by the above
cartoon.

Print answer here **HIS** "⦾⦾⦾⦾⦾" ⦾⦾⦾

JUMBLE®

Unscramble these four Jumbles, one letter to each square, to form four ordinary words.

GUGOE

GOLIO

ENBARN

NIANIZ

He can't carry a note

He can't carry a pail of water

No! No! No!

WHAT THE RIVAL TENORS WERE GOOD AT.

Now arrange the circled letters to form the surprise answer, as suggested by the above cartoon.

Print answer here

JUMBLE®

Unscramble these four Jumbles, one letter to each square, to form four ordinary words.

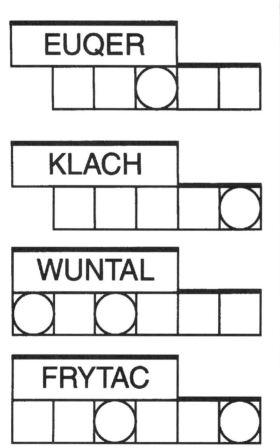

EUQER

KLACH

WUNTAL

FRYTAC

We'll skip the plumber and pay the doctor

HOW THE COUPLE PAID THEIR BILLS WHEN THEY RAN INTO MONEY WOES.

Now arrange the circled letters to form the surprise answer, as suggested by the above cartoon.

Print answer here

JUMBLE®

Unscramble these four Jumbles, one letter to each square, to form four ordinary words.

VAINE

VREEV

FEETOF

SEMIED

That's $50,000

It will grow in value

PEOPLE WHO HAVE ALL THE MONEY THEY NEED OFTEN GO AFTER THIS.

Now arrange the circled letters to form the surprise answer, as suggested by the above cartoon.

Print answer here

JUMBLE®

Unscramble these four Jumbles, one letter to each square, to form four ordinary words.

LITUB

DURIL

ELLGAY

TETINY

The dog ate my homework

Should I believe you?

FIBBING CAN TURN INTO THIS.

Now arrange the circled letters to form the surprise answer, as suggested by the above cartoon.

Print answer here A " ⬡⬡⬡ " ⬡⬡⬡⬡⬡⬡⬡⬡

JUMBLE®

Unscramble these four Jumbles, one letter to each square, to form four ordinary words.

HEEPS

MAITY

TARRMY

KILLEY

Did I tell you the one about ...

They've all heard it

IN HER EYES HUBBY'S OLD JOKES MADE HIM THIS.

Now arrange the circled letters to form the surprise answer, as suggested by the above cartoon.

Print answer here

A " ⬡⬡⬡⬡⬡ " ⬡⬡⬡⬡

JUMBLE®

Unscramble these four Jumbles, one letter to each square, to form four ordinary words.

DESET

CAMPH

PRETOY

LUGGEJ

Watch your grip

LEARNING TO BE A TRAPEZE ARTIST CAN BE THIS.

Now arrange the circled letters to form the surprise answer, as suggested by the above cartoon.

Print answer here [⃝⃝⃝⃝⃝] TO [⃝⃝⃝⃝⃝]

JUMBLE®

Unscramble these four Jumbles, one letter to
each square, to form four ordinary words.

FEZOR

TILIM

LIPPUT

FLUTAR

This one's so exciting

WHY SHE WANTED
A DRESS WITH
LOTS OF RUFFLES.

Now arrange the circled letters to form the
surprise answer, as suggested by the above
cartoon.

*Print
answer
here* **FOR
THE**

JUMBLE®

Unscramble these four Jumbles, one letter to
each square, to form four ordinary words.

OPYPP

OPUCE

TOPATE

GEDDER

Same color?

Try another one.
Anything's better

A DECISION AT
THE BEAUTY SHOP
OFTEN AMOUNTS
TO THIS.

Now arrange the circled letters to form the
surprise answer, as suggested by the above
cartoon.

Print answer here ⌐□○○□ **OR** □○○○□

JUMBLE®

Unscramble these four Jumbles, one letter to each square, to form four ordinary words.

TOLCH

DROAH

UNTRIP

NITIVE

He looks ten years younger

WHERE A TOUPEE CAN SUDDENLY APPEAR.

Now arrange the circled letters to form the surprise answer, as suggested by the above cartoon.

Print answer here ☐☐☐ OF ☐☐☐☐☐ ☐☐☐☐☐

JUMBLE®

Unscramble these four Jumbles, one letter to each square, to form four ordinary words.

TUMOH

PAKKO

AFDACE

CYGERL

Where's my order?

Relax, it's coming

THE LAZY CHEF'S SPECIALTY.

Now arrange the circled letters to form the surprise answer, as suggested by the above cartoon.

Print answer here " "

JUMBLE®

Unscramble these four Jumbles, one letter to each square, to form four ordinary words.

OSKET

FRUOM

FABFEL

RIVFEY

Hi, Herb

Nice wheels

A GOOD THING TO SEE IN A NEW CAR.

Now arrange the circled letters to form the surprise answer, as suggested by the above cartoon.

Print answer here

JUMBLE®

Unscramble these four Jumbles, one letter to
each square, to form four ordinary words.

WHISS

DUNOB

SICCEN

WHYTOR

I disagree! On
the other hand ...

WHAT THE FAST-
TALKING POLITICIAN
TOOK IN THE
DEBATE.

Now arrange the circled letters to form the
surprise answer, as suggested by the above
cartoon.

Print answer here

JUMBLE

Unscramble these four Jumbles, one letter to each square, to form four ordinary words.

TIBUC

INWET

NEXETT

BERICK

Anyone got any tape?

FOUND IN MANY CROCHET GROUPS.

Now arrange the circled letters to form the surprise answer, as suggested by the above cartoon.

Print answer here **A** ⬡⬡⬡⬡⬡ ⬡⬡⬡

JUMBLE®

Unscramble these four Jumbles, one letter to each square, to form four ordinary words.

YEMON

COUNE

TALMED

SADLIM

It looks perfect on her

She's such a pro

SHE WAS IN DEMAND FOR FASHION SHOWS BECAUSE SHE WAS ―――

Now arrange the circled letters to form the surprise answer, as suggested by the above cartoon.

Print answer here A

125

JUMBLE®

Unscramble these four Jumbles, one letter to each square, to form four ordinary words.

YENAH

CEKEH

SYPEDE

BOGENY

Your plan will ruin us!

Baloney!

HARD TO DO WHEN YOU GO HEAD TO HEAD.

Now arrange the circled letters to form the surprise answer, as suggested by the above cartoon.

Print answer here ◯◯◯ ◯◯◯ TO ◯◯◯

JUMBLE®

Unscramble these four Jumbles, one letter to
each square, to form four ordinary words.

RASCY

YOHEN

TANECC

RIVLIE

Both of you —
STOP
RIGHT
NOW!!

INEVITABLY RAISED
BY MOTHERS.

Now arrange the circled letters to form the
surprise answer, as suggested by the above
cartoon.

*Print
answer
here*

JUMBLE®

Unscramble these four Jumbles, one letter to each square, to form four ordinary words.

ACNIP

GINVY

RACLIG

NATFUL

Makes me feel super

WORKING OUT WITH WEIGHTS CAN BE THIS.

Now arrange the circled letters to form the surprise answer, as suggested by the above cartoon.

Print answer here

JUMBLE®

Unscramble these four Jumbles, one letter to
each square, to form four ordinary words.

CHEEN

CAUDT

SHEERA

SHULOC

WHAT THE MISER
CONSIDERED HIS
MATTRESS.

Now arrange the circled letters to form the
surprise answer, as suggested by the above
cartoon.

Print answer
here **A**

JUMBLE®

Unscramble these four Jumbles, one letter to each square, to form four ordinary words.

HERIK

ENCIE

HALDER

KAJECT

Eat lots of fruit and vegetables

It must be easier for her

THIS HELPED THEM LOSE WEIGHT.

Now arrange the circled letters to form the surprise answer, as suggested by the above cartoon.

Print answer **A** here

" "

JUMBLE®

Unscramble these four Jumbles, one letter to each square, to form four ordinary words.

SARBS

RYKUM

PARTTE

DOLITS

This theory is easily explained

$E=mc^2$

He sure knows his stuff

THE CLASS GENIUS DIDN'T DO THIS.

Now arrange the circled letters to form the surprise answer, as suggested by the above cartoon.

Print answer here " "

JUMBLE®

Unscramble these four Jumbles, one letter to each square, to form four ordinary words.

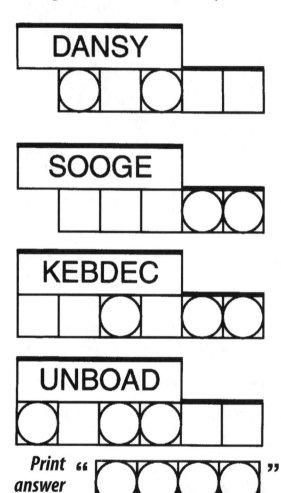

DANSY

SOOGE

KEBDEC

UNBOAD

Ha ha, missed me

IT BEGINS WITH THE FIRST SNOWBALL

Now arrange the circled letters to form the surprise answer, as suggested by the above cartoon.

Print answer here " "

JUMBLE®

Unscramble these four Jumbles, one letter to each square, to form four ordinary words.

SURVI

ZOTAP

SPUGMY

LEPPUR

They're incompetent

WHAT THE WINE MAKER WAS LEFT WITH WHEN HE LOST THE TASTE TEST.

Now arrange the circled letters to form the surprise answer, as suggested by the above cartoon.

Print answer here

JUMBLE®

Unscramble these four Jumbles, one letter to each square, to form four ordinary words.

BLYUL

TAUCE

POOSUR

FLACIE

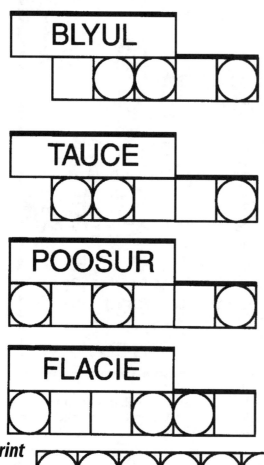

He's so good looking   And rich, too

HER INTEREST IN THE MILLIONAIRE WAS ——

Now arrange the circled letters to form the surprise answer, as suggested by the above cartoon.

Print answer here

JUMBLE®

Unscramble these four Jumbles, one letter to each square, to form four ordinary words.

SABUQ

SIGEE

STOMED

LAASSI

All we need are more customers

WHAT HE ENDED UP WITH WHEN HE INVESTED IN A BAR.

Now arrange the circled letters to form the surprise answer, as suggested by the above cartoon.

Print answer here

JUMBLE®

Unscramble these four Jumbles, one letter to
each square, to form four ordinary words.

DOITT

NAHVE

INDUPT

DALCUN

No more than 1200
calories a day

A GOOD PLACE
TO GO WHEN
YOU GAIN A
FEW POUNDS.

Now arrange the circled letters to form the
surprise answer, as suggested by the above
cartoon.

Print answer here ⬡⬡ A ⬡⬡⬡⬡

JUMBLE®

Unscramble these four Jumbles, one letter to each square, to form four ordinary words.

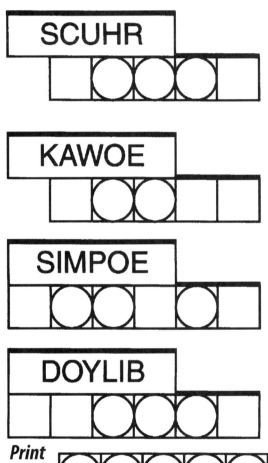

SCUHR

KAWOE

SIMPOE

DOYLIB

Keep them together. Take your time.

WHAT SHE RECEIVED FROM THE EXPERIENCED KNITTER.

Now arrange the circled letters to form the surprise answer, as suggested by the above cartoon.

Print answer here

OF

JUMBLE®

Unscramble these four Jumbles, one letter to
each square, to form four ordinary words.

SWEYN

GYTAN

HARKEW

STURME

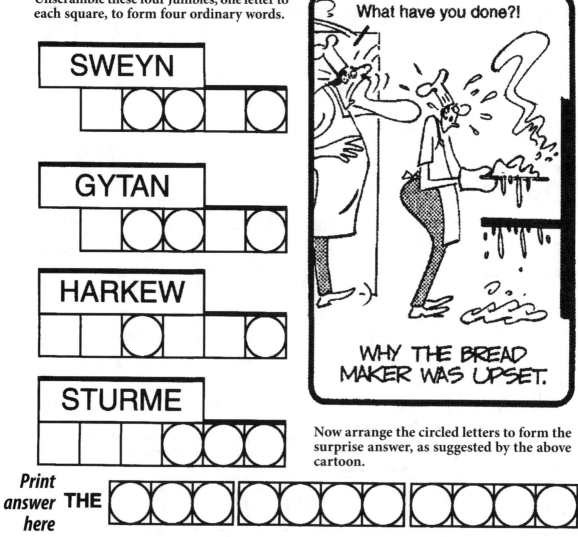

What have you done?!

WHY THE BREAD
MAKER WAS UPSET.

Now arrange the circled letters to form the
surprise answer, as suggested by the above
cartoon.

Print
answer **THE**
here

JUMBLE®

Unscramble these four Jumbles, one letter to
each square, to form four ordinary words.

TRUIF

YOGGS

ANOMEY

RICION

WHAT THE RACERS
WERE DOING
BEFORE THE FLAG
DROPPED.

Now arrange the circled letters to form the
surprise answer, as suggested by the above
cartoon.

Print
answer
here

" ⭕⭕⭕⭕⭕⭕⭕ " TO ⭕⭕

JUMBLE®

Unscramble these four Jumbles, one letter to
each square, to form four ordinary words.

NIGGO

CULOT

NANTIE

YOSSIF

Let's go over these
pages again

IMPORTANT FOR A
PODIATRY STUDENT
TO STUDY.

Now arrange the circled letters to form the
surprise answer, as suggested by the above
cartoon.

*Print answer
here* THE ⬡⬡⬡⬡⬡⬡⬡⬡⬡

JUMBLE®

Unscramble these four Jumbles, one letter to
each square, to form four ordinary words.

POANI

SMIPK

DUTILE

QUETEA

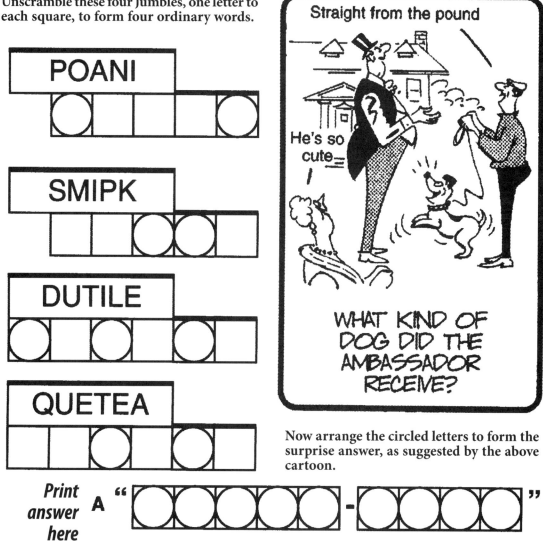

Straight from the pound

He's so cute

WHAT KIND OF
DOG DID THE
AMBASSADOR
RECEIVE?

Now arrange the circled letters to form the
surprise answer, as suggested by the above
cartoon.

*Print
answer
here*

A "◯◯◯◯◯-◯◯◯◯"

JUMBLE

Unscramble these four Jumbles, one letter to
each square, to form four ordinary words.

SVORI

NELEK

SEPPIN

HEHRST

I couldn't
do that

Takes great
balance

NEEDED BY AN
IRON WORKER.

Now arrange the circled letters to form the
surprise answer, as suggested by the above
cartoon.

Print
answer
here

⃝⃝⃝⃝⃝⃝ OF ⃝⃝⃝⃝⃝

JUMBLE®

Unscramble these four Jumbles, one letter to
each square, to form four ordinary words.

FRADT

LYDOM

DIRNEH

VINTAY

Elmer, is that you?   Where are your
overalls?

WHAT THE FIX-IT
MAN TURNED
INTO ON HIS
NIGHT OUT.

Now arrange the circled letters to form the
surprise answer, as suggested by the above
cartoon.

**Print
answer
here** A

JUMBLE®

Unscramble these four Jumbles, one letter to each square, to form four ordinary words.

AIZME

VALGE

BOTHED

THANYS

OFTEN THOUGHT BY A CONFIDENT PURSE SELLER.

Now arrange the circled letters to form the surprise answer, as suggested by the above cartoon.

Print answer here "◯◯ '◯ IN ◯◯◯ ◯◯◯"

JUMBLE®

Unscramble these four Jumbles, one letter to each square, to form four ordinary words.

TCHEF

TARAL

PHYSEC

YISMAL

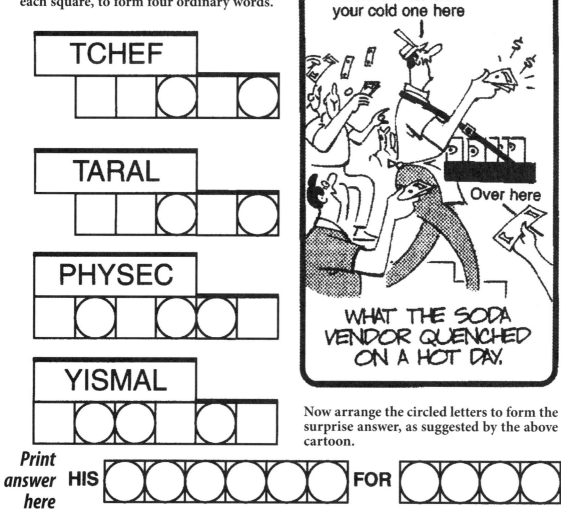

Cold drinks. Get your cold one here

Over here

WHAT THE SODA VENDOR QUENCHED ON A HOT DAY.

Now arrange the circled letters to form the surprise answer, as suggested by the above cartoon.

Print answer here HIS ⬡⬡⬡⬡⬡⬡ FOR ⬡⬡⬡⬡

JUMBLE®

Unscramble these four Jumbles, one letter to
each square, to form four ordinary words.

LOFOR

DUGOH

TASHAG

CREEFI

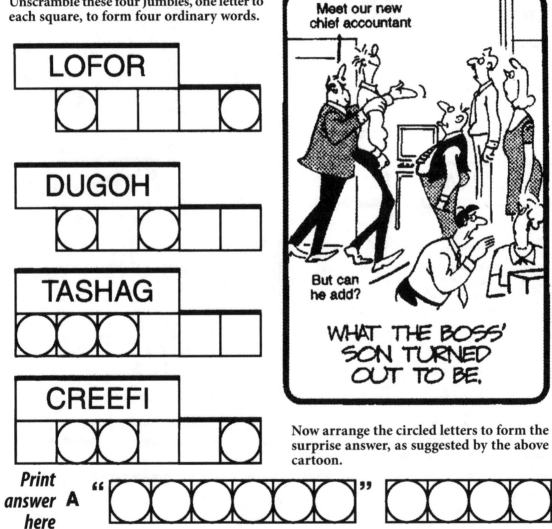

Meet our new
chief accountant

But can
he add?

WHAT THE BOSS'
SON TURNED
OUT TO BE.

Now arrange the circled letters to form the
surprise answer, as suggested by the above
cartoon.

*Print
answer* **A** " ◯◯◯◯◯◯ " ◯◯◯◯
here

JUMBLE®

Unscramble these four Jumbles, one letter to each square, to form four ordinary words.

PAUNC

TUPER

KEBTUC

PINGYT

She drives fast

Seat belts, everyone

MOM'S MINIVAN WAS KNOWN FOR THIS.

Now arrange the circled letters to form the surprise answer, as suggested by the above cartoon.

Print answer here **ITS** " ⬡⬡⬡⬡ ⬡⬡ "

JUMBLE®

Unscramble these four Jumbles, one letter to each square, to form four ordinary words.

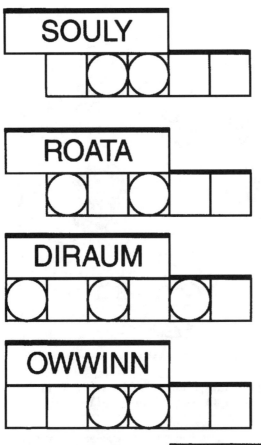

SOULY

ROATA

DIRAUM

OWWINN

Well, will you marry me?

We'll talk

WHAT SHE GOT FROM THE TRACK STAR.

Now arrange the circled letters to form the surprise answer, as suggested by the above cartoon.

Print answer here

JUMBLE®

Unscramble these four Jumbles, one letter to each square, to form four ordinary words.

VATLE

APLLE

HINGKT

KEPCAT

Time is up, here's your bill

EASILY REALIZED BY A VISIT TO A PSYCHIATRIST.

Now arrange the circled letters to form the surprise answer, as suggested by the above cartoon.

Print answer here ⬡⬡⬡⬡ **ISN'T** ⬡⬡⬡⬡⬡

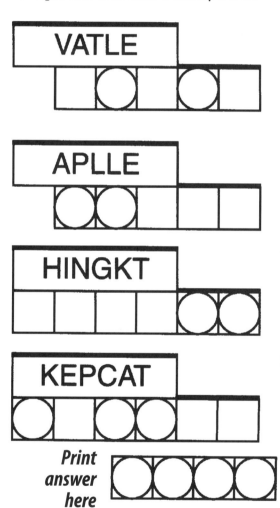

JUMBLE®

Unscramble these four Jumbles, one letter to each square, to form four ordinary words.

UPOHC

SITOC

CHYPIS

INTADE

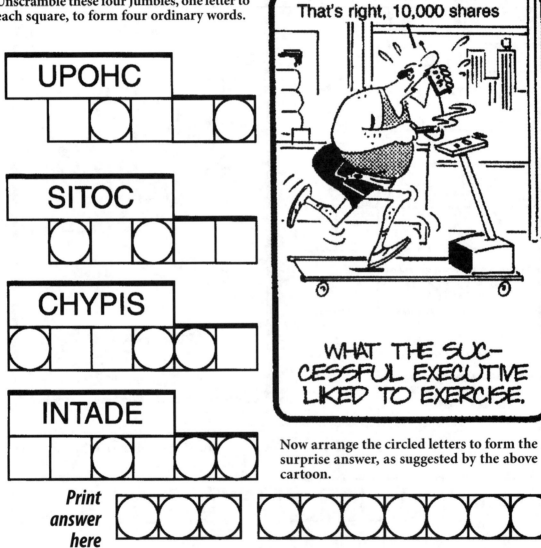

That's right, 10,000 shares

WHAT THE SUC-
CESSFUL EXECUTIVE
LIKED TO EXERCISE.

Now arrange the circled letters to form the surprise answer, as suggested by the above cartoon.

Print answer here

JUMBLE®

Unscramble these four Jumbles, one letter to each square, to form four ordinary words.

DUXEE

UVESA

ZARABA

MEENAC

He's awful

So was the last guy

THE KIND OF POETRY HEARD AT THE COFFEEHOUSE.

Now arrange the circled letters to form the surprise answer, as suggested by the above cartoon.

Print answer here

FROM ◯◯◯ TO ◯◯◯◯◯

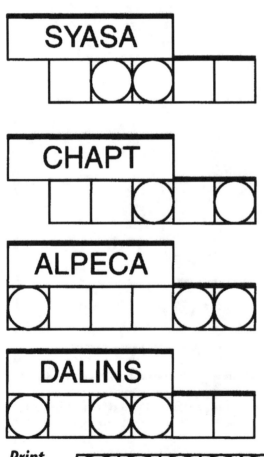

JUMBLE®

Unscramble these four Jumbles, one letter to each square, to form four ordinary words.

SYASA

CHAPT

ALPECA

DALINS

He says he'll double our money

Are you sure?

Play ball

WHAT THE CATCHER DISCUSSED WITH THE CURVE BALL ARTIST.

Now arrange the circled letters to form the surprise answer, as suggested by the above cartoon.

Print answer here

A ⬡⬡⬡⬡⬡ " ⬡⬡⬡⬡⬡ "

JUMBLE®

Unscramble these four Jumbles, one letter to each square, to form four ordinary words.

REDOO

SHAMC

SQUOME

OSANTA

Where's the beat?

WHEN MOM AND DAD DID THE TWO-STEP JUNIOR THOUGHT IT WAS THIS.

Now arrange the circled letters to form the surprise answer, as suggested by the above cartoon.

Print answer here   A "◯◯◯◯◯◯" ◯◯◯◯◯

JUMBLE®

Unscramble these four Jumbles, one letter to each square, to form four ordinary words.

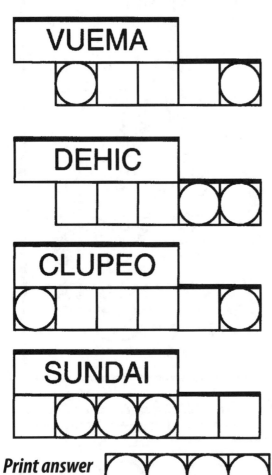

VUEMA

DEHIC

CLUPEO

SUNDAI

That's awful!

WHAT THE TEMPERAMENTAL STREET ARTIST DID.

Now arrange the circled letters to form the surprise answer, as suggested by the above cartoon.

Print answer here ⬡⬡⬡⬡ A " ⬡⬡⬡⬡⬡ "

JUMBLE®

Unscramble these four Jumbles, one letter to
each square, to form four ordinary words.

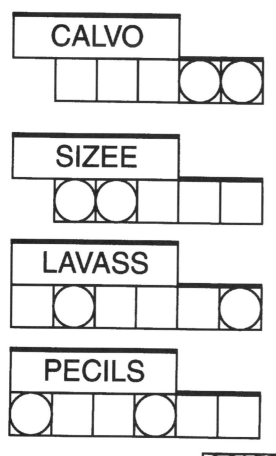

CALVO

SIZEE

LAVASS

PECILS

50% OFF

This is
our finest
canvas

WHERE THE
YACHTSMAN GOT
NEW RIGGING.

Now arrange the circled letters to form the
surprise answer, as suggested by the above
cartoon.

Print answer here **AT A**

JUMBLE®

Unscramble these four Jumbles, one letter to
each square, to form four ordinary words.

SCAMK

DONUP

KOOCIE

CAMIAN

I've
had it

Shift's
almost
over
!

WHAT THE
TIRED FRUIT
PICKERS WERE
READY TO DO.

Now arrange the circled letters to form the
surprise answer, as suggested by the above
cartoon.

Print answer here ◯◯◯◯ IT ◯◯

JUMBLE

Unscramble these four Jumbles, one letter to each square, to form four ordinary words.

YILSK

PEECA

GLEMIN

NERUNG

... and she was followed by Queen Isabella ...

WHAT THE STU- DENT OF ROYAL HISTORY STUDIED IN MADRID.

Now arrange the circled letters to form the surprise answer, as suggested by the above cartoon.

Print answer here **THE** ◯◯◯◯◯ **IN** ◯◯◯◯◯

JUMBLE®

Unscramble these four Jumbles, one letter to each square, to form four ordinary words.

TYFFI

ZAUER

LOMBAG

DEFROC

I'm getting a headache

THEY SAID THE
LOUD MUSIC IN
THE EXERCISE
CLASS WAS ----

Now arrange the circled letters to form the surprise answer, as suggested by the above cartoon.

Print answer here " ◯◯◯◯◯◯◯ "

JUMBLE®

Unscramble these four Jumbles, one letter to each square, to form four ordinary words.

BASSY

SOLOE

SCULIE

MARROD

Hurry, we leave in ten minutes

— I'm late

WHAT A BUSY MOM OFTEN DOES IN THE MORNING.

Now arrange the circled letters to form the surprise answer, as suggested by the above cartoon.

Print answer here

JUMBLE®

Unscramble these four Jumbles, one letter to each square, to form four ordinary words.

LORGY

KOPER

UPDYTE

IMCUPE

I'm never eating again

Leftovers, anyone?

HOW MANY END A THANKSGIVING BINGE.

Now arrange the circled letters to form the surprise answer, as suggested by the above cartoon.

Print answer here

JUMBLE®

Unscramble these four Jumbles, one letter to each square, to form four ordinary words.

LANVA

DUCIL

DAYPOR

OIDING

WE USE FRESH BEANS

The routine never changes

WORKING IN A COFFEEHOUSE IS OFTEN THIS.

Now arrange the circled letters to form the surprise answer, as suggested by the above cartoon.

Print answer here A ⬡⬡⬡⬡⬡⬡ ⬡⬡⬡⬡⬡

JUMBLE®

Unscramble these four Jumbles, one letter to each square, to form four ordinary words.

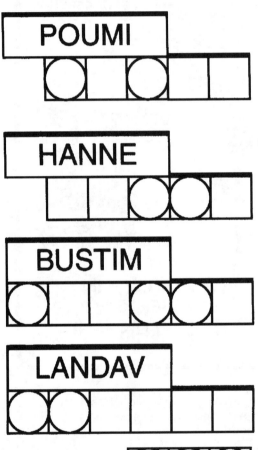

POUMI

HANNE

BUSTIM

LANDAV

I'm thinking of opening up a chain

A-E-I-O-U

E

THE OPTOMETRIST BECAME RICH BECAUSE HE WAS ---

Now arrange the circled letters to form the surprise answer, as suggested by the above cartoon.

Print answer here A ⃝⃝⃝ OF ⃝⃝⃝⃝⃝⃝⃝

JUMBLE Genius

Challenger Puzzles

JUMBLE®

Unscramble these six Jumbles, one letter to each square, to form six ordinary words.

REMIPE

EMBACE

YIRAWA

KUPPEE

OOGLYD

DETHOB

WHAT SHE SANG
AFTER SHE CHANGED
THE BABY'S DIAPERS.

Now arrange the circled letters to form the surprise answer, as suggested by the above cartoon.

Print answer here

" ⬡⬡⬡⬡ A ⬡⬡⬡ ⬡⬡⬡⬡ "

JUMBLE

Unscramble these six Jumbles, one letter to each square, to form six ordinary words.

LICIAT

GIRLYS

PIMAGE

HALMYN

INJOAD

PRUKAM

Capture their intensity

HOW THE DIRECTOR DESCRIBED THE ARM-WRESTLING MATCH.

Now arrange the circled letters to form the surprise answer, as suggested by the above cartoon.

Print answer here

A " ⬡⬡⬡⬡⬡⬡⬡ " ⬡⬡⬡⬡⬡

JUMBLE®

Unscramble these six Jumbles, one letter to
each square, to form six ordinary words.

WYIHNN

HIPLAC

RAUBIL

BLENGO

EECCAD

KABREY

Print answer here

" ◯◯◯◯◯ " ◯◯◯◯◯◯◯

Whoops!

They need
more lessons

A CLUMSY TANGO
CAN TURN INTO
THIS.

Now arrange the circled letters to form the
surprise answer, as suggested by the above
cartoon.

JUMBLE

Unscramble these six Jumbles, one letter to each square, to form six ordinary words.

CINANE

CUSCOT

SHATAM

CLAUHN

INFISH

EXYONG

It's 35 below

I've seen worse

BELOW-ZERO WEATHER MEANS THIS TO A VETERAN WEATHERMAN.

Now arrange the circled letters to form the surprise answer, as suggested by the above cartoon.

Print answer here

JUMBLE®

Unscramble these six Jumbles, one letter to each square, to form six ordinary words.

TRONIA

THOUPS

DUBACT

DULBOY

VORAYS

VIEWLS

It gives me good support

THE REFUSE COLLECTOR SAID HIS BACK BRACE WAS THIS.

Now arrange the circled letters to form the surprise answer, as suggested by the above cartoon.

Print answer here

A " ◯◯◯◯◯ " ◯◯◯◯◯◯◯

JUMBLE®

Unscramble these six Jumbles, one letter to each square, to form six ordinary words.

HYRITT

RAPPOL

NOBARC

ZEABAL

YENKOD

PRYSAT

Where you from? Are you working? I get so nervous ...

FEARED BY MANY SEATMATES ON DIRECT FLIGHTS.

Now arrange the circled letters to form the surprise answer, as suggested by the above cartoon.

Print answer here

A ⬡⬡⬡ - ⬡⬡⬡⬡ ⬡⬡⬡⬡⬡⬡

JUMBLE

Unscramble these six Jumbles, one letter to
each square, to form six ordinary words.

COORTH

STUMEK

FRYLUR

HERBTO

TALCOE

PRUNEY

I can't do it

WHAT THE NEW
CUB SCOUTS
ENDED UP WITH.

Now arrange the circled letters to form the
surprise answer, as suggested by the above
cartoon.

Print answer here

A

JUMBLE®

Unscramble these six Jumbles, one letter to
each square, to form six ordinary words.

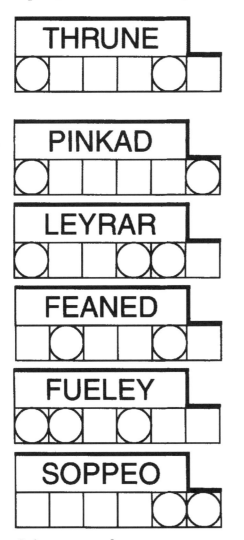

THRUNE

PINKAD

LEYRAR

FEANED

FUELEY

SOPPEO

You're
pretty

Do you like
my hair?

A VAIN BABYSITTER
WILL DO THIS.

Now arrange the circled letters to form the
surprise answer, as suggested by the above
cartoon.

Print answer here

AN ON

JUMBLE®

Unscramble these six Jumbles, one letter to
each square, to form six ordinary words.

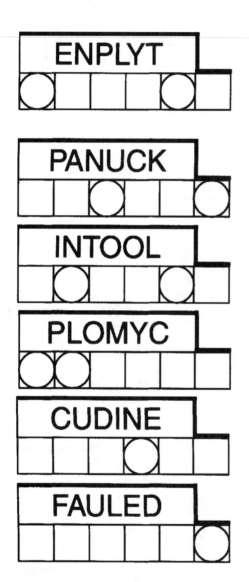

ENPLYT

PANUCK

INTOOL

PLOMYC

CUDINE

FAULED

Not now. I'm
working on
an idea

WHAT THE CHEF
HAD TO DO WHEN
HE DECIDED TO
WRITE A NOVEL.

Now arrange the circled letters to form the
surprise answer, as suggested by the above
cartoon.

**Print
answer
here**
 **A**

JUMBLE®

Unscramble these six Jumbles, one letter to each square, to form six ordinary words.

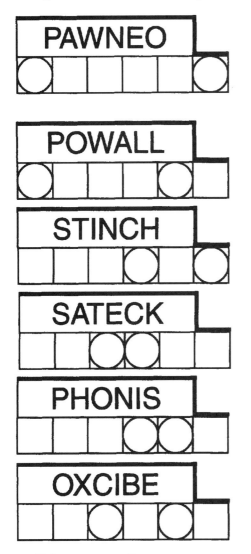

PAWNEO

POWALL

STINCH

SATECK

PHONIS

OXCIBE

He's an expert

WHY THEY ASKED THE MARKSMAN TO TAKE THE PHOTOS.

Now arrange the circled letters to form the surprise answer, as suggested by the above cartoon.

Print answer here

HE ⬡⬡⬡⬡⬡ ⬡⬡⬡ TO ⬡⬡⬡⬡⬡

JUMBLE®

Unscramble these six Jumbles, one letter to each square, to form six ordinary words.

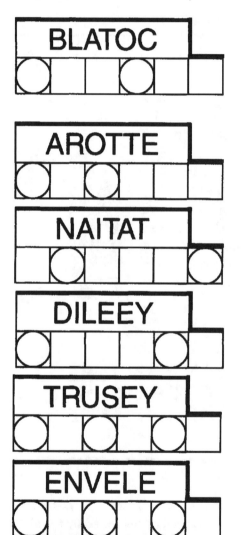

BLATOC

AROTTE

NAITAT

DILEEY

TRUSEY

ENVELE

Six percent   Sounds great

WHY THE BANKER OFFERED AN ATTRACTIVE MORTGAGE RATE.

Now arrange the circled letters to form the surprise answer, as suggested by the above cartoon.

Print answer here

TO

JUMBLE®

Unscramble these six Jumbles, one letter to each square, to form six ordinary words.

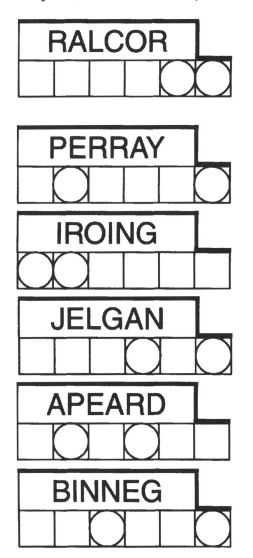

RALCOR

PERRAY

IROING

JELGAN

APEARD

BINNEG

Hope I can borrow the money

BANK

SALOON

WHO WAS TONTO LOOKING FOR IN THE BANK?

Now arrange the circled letters to form the surprise answer, as suggested by the above cartoon.

Print answer here

THE "  "

JUMBLE®

Unscramble these six Jumbles, one letter to each square, to form six ordinary words.

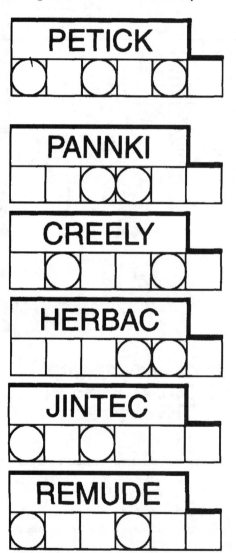

PETICK

PANNKI

CREELY

HERBAC

JINTEC

REMUDE

I'll fix it for $50

That's highway robbery

OFTEN THE RESULT OF AN EMERGENCY TIRE CHANGE.

Now arrange the circled letters to form the surprise answer, as suggested by the above cartoon.

Print answer here

A ⬡⬡⬡⬡⬡⬡-⬡⬡ ⬡⬡⬡⬡⬡

JUMBLE®

Unscramble these six Jumbles, one letter to
each square, to form six ordinary words.

GOURAC

FLITUE

TREETH

BLATUR

INFREY

NAPHOR

You have
my ace

Now he
reads minds

WHAT THE PSYCHIA-
TRISTS TURNED
THE COMMUTER
EXPRESS INTO.

Now arrange the circled letters to form the
surprise answer, as suggested by the above
cartoon.

Print answer here

A ⬡⬡⬡⬡⬡ OF " ⬡⬡⬡⬡⬡⬡⬡ "

JUMBLE®

Unscramble these six Jumbles, one letter to each square, to form six ordinary words.

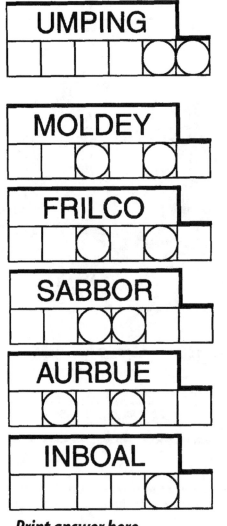

UMPING

MOLDEY

FRILCO

SABBOR

AURBUE

INBOAL

Print answer here

BUY ONE POUND, SECOND IS FREE

HOW THE PASTA MAKER INCREASED SALES.

Now arrange the circled letters to form the surprise answer, as suggested by the above cartoon.

BY ◯◯◯◯◯ HIS ◯◯◯◯◯◯

JUMBLE®

Unscramble these six Jumbles, one letter to each square, to form six ordinary words.

GROITE

MILGRY

SINOUF

HERTAH

DAHNED

BLOTTE

That's a good batch

THEY MADE THE MOONSHINE HERE.

Now arrange the circled letters to form the surprise answer, as suggested by the above cartoon.

Print answer here

◯◯◯ " ◯◯◯◯◯ " OF THE ◯◯◯◯◯◯

JUMBLE®

Unscramble these six Jumbles, one letter to each square, to form six ordinary words.

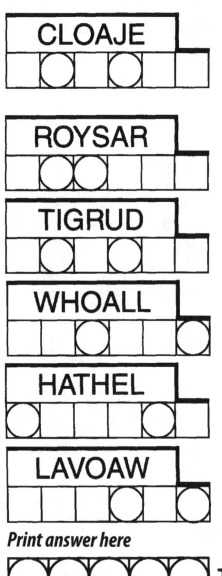

CLOAJE

ROYSAR

TIGRUD

WHOALL

HATHEL

LAVOAW

This is like cardboard

Er ... uh ... I think the chef is ... er ... sick today

HIS REASON FOR THE OVERCOOKED STEAK WAS THIS.

Now arrange the circled letters to form the surprise answer, as suggested by the above cartoon.

Print answer here

TO

JUMBLE®

Unscramble these six Jumbles, one letter to each square, to form six ordinary words.

INCLEY

NELPOL

REECCO

ENGALC

CADIVE

MYDIAS

You've caught the limit

EASY TO EXPERIENCE WHEN THE FISH ARE BITING.

Now arrange the circled letters to form the surprise answer, as suggested by the above cartoon.

Print answer here

A " ☐☐☐☐ " ☐☐☐☐ ☐☐☐

JUMBLE.

Unscramble these six Jumbles, one letter to each square, to form six ordinary words.

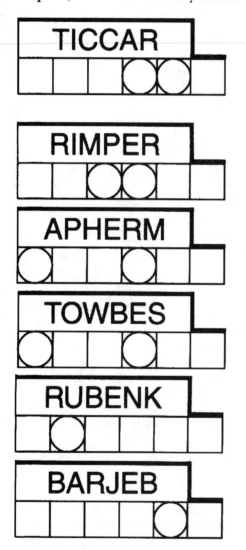

TICCAR

RIMPER

APHERM

TOWBES

RUBENK

BARJEB

Hey, Dad, can I have ten bucks for gas?

WHAT THE YOUNG DRACULA FIGURE DID TO DAD ON HALLOWEEN.

Now arrange the circled letters to form the surprise answer, as suggested by the above cartoon.

Print answer here

○○○ THE ○○○○○ ON ○○○

JUMBLE®

Unscramble these six Jumbles, one letter to
each square, to form six ordinary words.

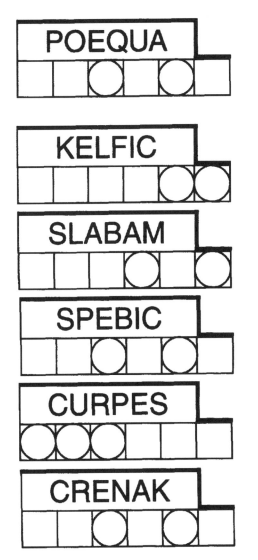

POEQUA

KELFIC

SLABAM

SPEBIC

CURPES

CRENAK

That's
scary

They're a
cut above
us

COLLEGE POLE
VAULTERS
BECOME THIS.

Now arrange the circled letters to form the
surprise answer, as suggested by the above
cartoon.

Print answer here

" ◯◯◯◯◯ " ◯◯◯◯◯◯◯◯

ANSWERS

1. **Jumbles:** PANSY CRAFT HUMBLE MEMBER
   Answer: What did they engrave on the robot's tombstone?—RUST IN PEACE

2. **Jumbles:** BASIS LAPEL HAMMER ALBINO
   Answer: Obligated according to law when you "concoct" a libel—"LIABLE"

3. **Jumbles:** FELON WAKEN MEADOW HORROR
   Answer: Present at present but not present—"NOW-HERE" (nowhere)

4. **Jumbles:** NEEDY USURY COMMON RADISH
   Answer: What she told her cowboy friend not to do—HORSE AROUND

5. **Jumbles:** WAGON KINKY SOCIAL DOUBLE
   Answer: What happened to the man who invented vanishing cream?—NOBODY KNOWS

6. **Jumbles:** HIKER FLOOD ENCAMP DELUXE
   Answer: What she told her husband he had better do while on that fishing trip—DROP A LINE

7. **Jumbles:** WALTZ UPPER KENNEL ANYWAY
   Answer: When he saw the cops, the robber took off and left his accomplice to do this—TAKE THE "WRAP"

8. **Jumbles:** APPLY BURLY FAMILY JUNGLE
   Answer: The kangaroo visited a shrink because he had been feeling this lately—JUMPY

9. **Jumbles:** BRIBE FLANK MODIFY ACTING
   Answer: When they invented drip-dry clothes, this just about came to an end—THE IRON AGE

10. **Jumbles:** PERKY WEDGE ARCADE EMERGE
    Answer: People who don't dye their hair could eventually do this—MAKE THE "GRAYED"

11. **Jumbles:** FLUKE CAMEO SAFARI DRAGON
    Answer: Frankenstein was lonely until he discovered how to do this—MAKE FRIENDS

12. **Jumbles:** POWER BLOAT FACIAL CLOVER
    Answer: What happened when he put dynamite into the refrigerator?—HE BLEW HIS COOL

13. **Jumbles:** VAPOR ELITE THORAX CIPHER
    Answer: Is it going to be a local or a general anesthetic?—"YOU CAN HAVE ETHER"

14. **Jumbles:** UTTER JUICE DURESS ADJOIN
    Answer: What the lawyer demanded to have with his drink—"JUST ICE"

15. **Jumbles:** FAIRY ENEMY PAUPER TALLOW
    Answer: What the ram said to the female of the species—I'M AFTER EWE

16. **Jumbles:** VENOM BRIAR OUTING HALLOW
    Answer: The miner didn't know whether he had struck this—IRON ORE WHAT

17. **Jumbles:** TEMPO UNCLE KOWTOW SHANTY
    Answer: Who's heard about the big kidnapping?—"HE WOKE UP"

18. **Jumbles:** LYRIC BULLY FORMAL PILFER
    Answer: How she slipped into her bikini—"BRIEF-LY"

19. **Jumbles:** HUMID GLAND TALKER HICCUP
    Answer: The goat ate an electric bulb because all he wanted was this—A LIGHT LUNCH

20. **Jumbles:** SNORT ALIAS SAILOR EXPOSE
    Answer: It was his last meal, but you should have seen this—HOW THE ASSASSINATE (assassin ate)

21. **Jumbles:** CEASE ALTAR BELLOW DEFACE
    Answer: The crooked architect discovered that prison walls weren't built this way—TO SCALE

22. **Jumbles:** FLOOR AFTER GALLEY BAFFLE
    Answer: He decided to retire after his performances began to do this—FALL OFF

23. **Jumbles:** TWINE FAITH BISHOP PLURAL
    Answer: The librarian also cried when she saw her books were this—IN "TIERS"

24. **Jumbles:** PECAN CURVE ATOMIC ORPHAN
    Answer: He was so broke that all the pickpocket got from him was this—PRACTICE

25. **Jumbles:** GOING DEMON PHYSIC FACADE
    Answer: What that mutt liked best for breakfast—"POOCHED" EGGS

26. **Jumbles:** ABHOR GLOAT STUCCO SHERRY
    Answer: Easy for a reporter to get at a doughnut shop—THE "HOLE" STORY

27. **Jumbles:** ELDER CRESS PREFER FLAXEN
    Answer: How she felt when the doctor said, "No problem, no charge"—CARE "FREE"

28. **Jumbles:** IDIOT FAULT ABLAZE ZEALOT
    Answer: This happened when he tried to drink a case of soda—HE "FIZZLED" OUT

29. **Jumbles:** TULIP BRAND BOUNTY BELONG
    Answer: How the show dog prepared for the competition—HE BONED UP

30. **Jumbles:** GUESS ESSAY RADISH PLURAL
    Answer: How the hot dog vendor tackled his job—WITH "RELISH"

31. **Jumbles:** LINER PURGE RATION BLEACH
    Answer: Why the company's president went back to school—FOR "HIRE" LEARNING

32. **Jumbles:** SUAVE MAJOR HARDLY RANCID
    Answer: What the department store clerks looked forward to—A JANUARY SAIL

33. **Jumbles:** PATIO HABIT RARITY EXPOSE
    Answer: Pilots and cab drivers have this in common—AIRPORT TAXIS

34. **Jumbles:** LOFTY GUMBO AIRWAY FITFUL
    Answer: What happened when the rooster was stopped for speeding—THE FOWL RAN AFOUL

35. **Jumbles:** CREEK SHYLY MEADOW ALWAYS
    Answer: How Mom felt while she darned socks—SEW-SEW

36. **Jumbles:** DECAY TYING SLEIGH CURFEW
    Answer: What the street thugs considered the whiz kid—A "WISE" GUY

37. **Jumbles:** DAILY CREEL ENCAMP CONVOY
    Answer: Why everyone wanted to stay at the popular hotel—IT WAS THE "INN" PLACE

38. **Jumbles:** IRATE PRIZE TURBAN ACTING
    Answer: What the global strategist focused on during his leisure time—THE BIG PICTURE

39. **Jumbles:** FENCE GIVEN ENGULF QUIVER
    Answer: A highly paid model will enjoy this—A NICE FIGURE

40. **Jumbles:** MOUNT LIGHT VERMIN JIGGER
    Answer: Why the old timer envied the young mechanic—HE WAS "RE-TIRING"

41. **Jumbles:** FACET GOURD RAVAGE BROOCH
    Answer: Needed to be a good soccer player—A HEAD FOR IT

42. **Jumbles:** GAMUT RUMMY SURTAX ENOUGH
    Answer: What backseat drivers never do—RUN OUT OF "GAS"

43. **Jumbles:** JOINT LIMBO KNOTTY HANGAR
    Answer: A good idea can lead to this—BIRTH OF A NOTION

44. **Jumbles:** GAUDY HEAVY LEGUME PROFIT
    Answer: What the bookkeepers considered their lazy boss—A "FIGURE" HEAD

45. **Jumbles:** AGILE ITCHY BEWAIL ENMITY
    Answer: Mom can do this over a dirty floor—HIT THE CEILING

46. **Jumbles:** HAIRY LOWLY IMBUED AUTUMN
    Answer: What the babysitter had when the infant got crabby—A "WAIL" OF A TIME

47. **Jumbles:** THYME IDIOT ADMIRE ALKALI
Answer: How the driver wanted his race car to perform—LIKE A DREAM

48. **Jumbles:** CABIN BEGOT MATRON SALUTE
Answer: What the coffee plantation owner needed—A BEAN COUNTER

49. **Jumbles:** ICILY INEPT MALICE RENEGE
Answer: How a late train on a cold morning left the commuters—RAILING

50. **Jumbles:** CRACK LOVER SCORCH THRASH
Answer: What the actor-turned-fisherman got from his date—THE HOOK

51. **Jumbles:** BRAND CABLE FIESTA CRAVAT
Answer: Getting sick at a rustic hideaway can leave you with—CABIN "FEVER"

52. **Jumbles:** OCCUR AWASH FERRET INFANT
Answer: Possessed by a calligrapher—THE WRITE STUFF

53. **Jumbles:** AGLOW WAGON CATTLE TUSSLE
Answer: What it takes to argue over a dance step—TWO TO TANGLE

54. **Jumbles:** BRAVO REBEL PAGODA OBLIGE
Answer: Useful when sneaking out for a round of golf—A GOOD LIE

55. **Jumbles:** FENCE STOOP RADIUS DEFACE
Answer: A strict diet gave him this—SIDE EFFECTS

56. **Jumbles:** GLOAT FETID VANISH MANAGE
Answer: What the fussy customer finally did to the salesman—GAVE HIM A FIT

57. **Jumbles:** GASSY UPPER AMBUSH TROUGH
Answer: How the hansom driver ended up when he caught a cold—HOARSE AND BUGGY

58. **Jumbles:** COCOA EXPEL TRUANT ECZEMA
Answer: How the balding manager fared in the race for the job—HE CAME OUT ON TOP

59. **Jumbles:** ESSAY OXIDE OUTBID UNTRUE
Answer: What the music student did before the test—STUDIED HIS "NOTES"

60. **Jumbles:** LYING AWFUL AVENUE INDOOR
Answer: How Mom ended up when Junior got into the sewing box—UNWOUND

61. **Jumbles:** LANKY ADULT KETTLE CHUBBY
Answer: A masseur gets a lot of this—BACK TALK

62. **Jumbles:** ARMOR LOUSE LAWFUL MODIFY
Answer: What he said to Dad when he flunked the spelling test—"WORDS FAIL ME"

63. **Jumbles:** MADAM MAXIM SLEEPY PELVIS
Answer: Why the horn player had the girls swooning—HE HAD SAX APPEAL

64. **Jumbles:** FRAUD GAILY WATERY HALVED
Answer: What they ended up with when they dove into the breakers—"WAVY" HAIR

65. **Jumbles:** THINK GUEST OPENLY FLAXEN
Answer: How Mom felt after her all-day shopping spree—"SPENT"

66. **Jumbles:** YOUTH PENCE FIASCO BRIDGE
Answer: What the dentist gave the TV reporter—A SOUND BITE

67. **Jumbles:** PRINT RHYME WEASEL GOLFER
Answer: Running on a treadmill will get you here—NOWHERE FAST

68. **Jumbles:** TARDY NOBLE TIDBIT BLAZER
Answer: Given to the horse that pulled the wedding carriage—A BRIDAL BRIDLE

69. **Jumbles:** LITHE WIPED EXHORT AFFIRM
Answer: Where the kids landed for playing in the mud—IN HOT WATER

70. **Jumbles:** KITTY ANKLE JERSEY WOBBLE
Answer: Why a building site is carefully measured—A "LOT" IS AT STAKE

71. **Jumbles:** MINOR PANSY GAMBIT GYRATE
Answer: Shopping for a new outfit usually results in this—"TRYING" TIMES

72. **Jumbles:** QUEST SOUSE NEWEST CAUCUS
Answer: What the young chef experienced when his dish became popular—A "TASTE" OF SUCCESS

73. **Jumbles:** JUROR CHIME MEMBER SHADOW
Answer: Another name for a tourist information center—A "WHERE" HOUSE

74. **Jumbles:** GNARL ELEGY POSTAL BOUNCE
Answer: The author said his wine collection was—A "BEST CELLAR"

75. **Jumbles:** ROUSE VIPER MOTIVE PESTLE
Answer: How he found the tattoo artist to be—IMPRESSIVE

76. **Jumbles:** POACH HONOR IMPORT GEYSER
Answer: What the restaurant on Mars lacked—ATMOSPHERE

77. **Jumbles:** UNWED TEMPO OCCULT PARISH
Answer: What the barber gave the sailors—"CREW" CUTS

78. **Jumbles:** FANCY ROBIN ARMORY BEAVER
Answer: This can occur when the alimony is late—ACRIMONY

79. **Jumbles:** CURVE RIGOR FROSTY NUMBER
Answer: Found at most hotels—BROOM SERVICE

80. **Jumbles:** PURGE SAUTE ENTICE ZENITH
Answer: What the self-centered optometrist gave his patient—"I" STRAIN

81. **Jumbles:** PANDA FAIRY JAILED HERMIT
Answer: What a carnival boss must always be—"FAIR" MINDED

82. **Jumbles:** PILOT HUMAN VALISE MILDEW
Answer: Where the clumsy helper left the chef—IN A STEW

83. **Jumbles:** MEALY BROIL BRIDLE REDEEM
Answer: The kind of business the catalog house got from men—"MALE" ORDER

84. **Jumbles:** EMERY ELOPE VORTEX NOODLE
Answer: The divers had an underwater wedding because they were—DEEPLY IN LOVE

85. **Jumbles:** GAWKY FOCUS TOWARD JAGGED
Answer: This happened when he bought an umbrella in the rain—HE GOT SOAKED

86. **Jumbles:** FOAMY CIVIL BEATEN SNAPPY
Answer: Why he altered her portrait—TO SAVE FACE

87. **Jumbles:** TESTY GLOVE DEADLY VIRTUE
Answer: Used to make wedding veils—TULLES OF THE TRADE

88. **Jumbles:** MESSY DINER DRAGON WINTRY
Answer: What he got from Mom for not dressing up—A DRESSING DOWN

89. **Jumbles:** CRIME MOOSE BUTLER NEARBY
Answer: A no-fat diet on a tight budget can lead to this—LEAN TIMES

90. **Jumbles:** HOUSE BIRCH UNCURL TYPHUS
Answer: What the barber gave the artist—A "BRUSH" CUT

91. **Jumbles:** LIVEN KEYED PLOWED HELPER
Answer: How he felt when his shoes were repaired—WELL HEELED

92. **Jumbles:** IMPEL NOVEL RELISH SIMILE
Answer: Useful tools for some solicitors—"SELL" PHONES

93. **Jumbles:** TOXIC PUPPY CRAYON FURROW
Answer: Where he stood on helping with the housework—OUT OF THE WAY

94. **Jumbles:** ORBIT BROOD COSTLY PIRATE
Answer: Another name for a high chair—A BABYSITTER

185

95. **Jumbles:** UNIFY FLOUR CODGER TAWDRY
Answer: How Mom felt after doing laundry all day—WRUNG OUT

96. **Jumbles:** PAUSE TRAIT PAUNCH CEMENT
Answer: What the cows watched during the marathon—THE HUMAN RACE

97. **Jumbles:** PROVE BUSHY WALRUS FELLOW
Answer: How the needlepoint instructor described her work—SEW-SEW

98. **Jumbles:** SNOWY CAMEO ADJUST COUSIN
Answer: You might call making preserves this—A JAM SESSION

99. **Jumbles:** FLANK GROOM SADIST PRISON
Answer: What the company hoped its new drug would cure—LOSS OF PROFIT

100. **Jumbles:** QUAIL YEARN POWDER CIPHER
Answer: Important for a gift of hip-hop music—A RAP WRAP

101. **Jumbles:** QUASH WEARY MEDLEY FUMBLE
Answer: What Dad did when he got the electric bill—BLEW A FUSE

102. **Jumbles:** BURLY SAVOR SHEKEL JITNEY
Answer: What the inept carpenter's helper tried to do—HIS "LEVEL" BEST

103. **Jumbles:** DEITY SINGE TRUDGE URCHIN
Answer: This can happen when a craps shooter loses—THINGS GET DICEY

104. **Jumbles:** PHOTO BROOK JUNGLE AFLOAT
Answer: Tough to do when suffering from laryngitis—TALK ABOUT IT

105. **Jumbles:** DIZZY FORCE GOODLY GARISH
Answer: What students experience after a long summer break—SCHOOL DAZE

106. **Jumbles:** IVORY POKED STRONG INFIRM
Answer: Snorkelers and mosquitoes have this in common—SKIN DIVING

107. **Jumbles:** EMPTY FIORD BEYOND ENCORE
Answer: What you need to thread a needle—AN EYE FOR IT

108. **Jumbles:** USURY MILKY POCKET NIBBLE
Answer: Where his resolution to stop using cigarettes went—UP IN SMOKE

109. **Jumbles:** HASTY WAFER VACUUM ADRIFT
Answer: His first shift at the sausage factory turned into this—HIS "WURST" DAY

110. **Jumbles:** GOUGE IGLOO BANNER ZINNIA
Answer: What the rival tenors were good at—ZINGING

111. **Jumbles:** QUEER CHALK WALNUT CRAFTY
Answer: How the couple paid their bills when they ran into money woes—WEAKLY

112. **Jumbles:** NAÏVE VERVE TOFFEE DEMISE
Answer: People who have all the money they need often go after this—EVEN MORE

113. **Jumbles:** BUILT LURID GALLEY ENTITY
Answer: Fibbing can turn into this—A "LIE" ABILITY

114. **Jumbles:** SHEEP AMITY MARTYR LIKELY
Answer: In her eyes hubby's old jokes made him this—A "STALE" MATE

115. **Jumbles:** STEED CHAMP POETRY JUGGLE
Answer: Learning to be a trapeze artist can be this—TOUGH TO GRASP

116. **Jumbles:** FROZE LIMIT PULPIT ARTFUL
Answer: Why she wanted a dress with lots of ruffles—FOR THE FRILL OF IT

117. **Jumbles:** POPPY COUPE TEAPOT DREDGE
Answer: A decision at the beauty shop often amounts to this—'DO OR DYE

118. **Jumbles:** CLOTH HOARD TURNIP INVITE
Answer: Where a toupee can suddenly appear—OUT OF THIN HAIR

119. **Jumbles:** MOUTH KAPOK FAÇADE CLERGY
Answer: The lazy chef's specialty—MEAT "LOAF"

120. **Jumbles:** STOKE FORUM BAFFLE VERIFY
Answer: A good thing to see in a new car—YOURSELF

121. **Jumbles:** SWISH BOUND SCENIC WORTHY
Answer: What the fast-talking politician took in the debate—BOTH SIDES

122. **Jumbles:** CUBIT TWINE EXTENT BICKER
Answer: Found in many crochet groups—A KNIT WIT

123. **Jumbles:** MONEY OUNCE MALTED DISMAL
Answer: She was in demand for fashion shows because she was—A MODEL MODEL

124. **Jumbles:** HYENA CHEEK SPEEDY BYGONE
Answer: Hard to do when you go head to head—SEE EYE TO EYE

125. **Jumbles:** SCARY HONEY ACCENT VIRILE
Answer: Inevitably raised by mothers—THEIR VOICES

126. **Jumbles:** PANIC VYING GARLIC FLAUNT
Answer: Working out with weights can be this—UPLIFTING

127. **Jumbles:** HENCE DUCAT HEARSE SLOUCH
Answer: What the miser considered his mattress—A CASH CACHE

128. **Jumbles:** HIKER NIECE HERALD JACKET
Answer: This helped them lose weight—A HEALTH "KICK"

129. **Jumbles:** BRASS MURKY PATTER STOLID
Answer: The class genius didn't do this—DRESS "SMARTLY"

130. **Jumbles:** SANDY GOOSE BEDECK ABOUND
Answer: It begins with the first snowball—"DUCK" SEASON

131. **Jumbles:** VIRUS TOPAZ GYPSUM PURPLE
Answer: What the wine maker was left with when he lost the taste test—SOUR GRAPES

132. **Jumbles:** BULLY ACUTE POROUS FACILE
Answer: Her interest in the millionaire was—PURELY FISCAL

133. **Jumbles:** SQUAB SIEGE MODEST ASSAIL
Answer: What he ended up with when he invested in a bar—LIQUID ASSETS

134. **Jumbles:** DITTO HAVEN PUNDIT UNCLAD
Answer: A good place to go when you gain a few pounds—ON A DIET

135. **Jumbles:** CRUSH AWOKE IMPOSE BODILY
Answer: What she received from the experienced knitter—PURLS OF WISDOM

136. **Jumbles:** NEWSY TANGY HAWKER MUSTER
Answer: Why the bread maker was upset—THE RYE WENT AWRY

137. **Jumbles:** FRUIT SOGGY YEOMAN IRONIC
Answer: What the racers were doing before the flag dropped—"ROARING" TO GO

138. **Jumbles:** GOING CLOUT INNATE OSSIFY
Answer: Important for a podiatry student to study—THE FOOTNOTES

139. **Jumbles:** PIANO SKIMP DILUTE EQUATE
Answer: What kind of dog did the ambassador receive?—A "DIPLO-MUTT"

140. **Jumbles:** VISOR KNEEL PEPSIN THRESH
Answer: Needed by an iron worker—NERVES OF STEEL

141. **Jumbles:** DRAFT MOLDY HINDER VANITY
Answer: What the fix-it man turned into on his night out—A HANDY DANDY

142. **Jumbles:** MAIZE GAVEL HOTBED SHANTY
Answer: Often thought by a confident purse seller—"IT'S IN THE BAG"

143. **Jumbles:** FETCH ALTAR PSYCHE MISLAY
Answer: What the soda vendor quenched on a hot day—HIS THIRST FOR CASH

144. **Jumbles:** FLOOR DOUGH AGHAST FIERCE
Answer: What the boss' son turned out to be—
A "FIGURE" HEAD

145. **Jumbles:** UNCAP ERUPT BUCKET TYPING
Answer: Mom's minivan was known for this—
ITS "PICK UP"

146. **Jumbles:** LOUSY AORTA RADIUM WINNOW
Answer: What she got from the track star—
RUNAROUND

147. **Jumbles:** VALET LAPEL KNIGHT PACKET
Answer: Easily realized by a visit to a psychiatrist—
TALK ISN'T CHEAP

148. **Jumbles:** POUCH STOIC PHYSIC DETAIN
Answer: What the successful executive liked to
exercise—HIS OPTIONS

149. **Jumbles:** EXUDE SUAVE BAZAAR MENACE
Answer: The kind of poetry heard at the coffeehouse—
FROM BAD TO VERSE

150. **Jumbles:** ASSAY PATCH PALACE ISLAND
Answer: What the catcher discussed with the curve ball
artist—A SALES "PITCH"

151. **Jumbles:** RODEO CHASM MOSQUE SONATA
Answer: When Mom and Dad did the two-step Junior
thought it was this—A "SQUARE" DANCE

152. **Jumbles:** MAUVE CHIDE COUPLE UNSAID
Answer: What the temperamental street artist did—
MADE A "SCENE"

153. **Jumbles:** VOCAL SEIZE VASSAL SPLICE
Answer: Where the yachtsman got new rigging—
AT A SAIL SALE

154. **Jumbles:** SMACK POUND COOKIE MANIAC
Answer: What the tired fruit pickers were ready to
do—PACK IT IN

155. **Jumbles:** SILKY PEACE MINGLE GUNNER
Answer: What the student of royal history studied in
Madrid—THE REIGN IN SPAIN

156. **Jumbles:** FIFTY AZURE GAMBOL FORCED
Answer: They said the loud music in the exercise class
was—"EAROBIC"

157. **Jumbles:** ABYSS LOOSE SLUICE RAMROD
Answer: What a busy mom often does in the
morning—SCRAMBLES

158. **Jumbles:** GLORY POKER DEPUTY PUMICE
Answer: How many end a Thanksgiving binge—
COLD TURKEY

159. **Jumbles:** NAVAL LUCID PARODY INDIGO
Answer: Working in a coffeehouse is often this—
A DAILY GRIND

160. **Jumbles:** OPIUM HENNA SUBMIT VANDAL
Answer: The optometrist became rich because he
was—A MAN OF VISION

161. **Jumbles:** EMPIRE BECAME AIRWAY UPKEEP
GOODLY HOTBED
Answer: What she sang after she changed the baby's
diapers—"ROCK A DRY BABY"

162. **Jumbles:** ITALIC GRISLY MAGPIE HYMNAL
ADJOIN MARKUP
Answer: How the director described the arm-wrestling
match—A "GRIPPING" DRAMA

163. **Jumbles:** WHINNY CALIPH BURIAL BELONG
ACCEDE BAKERY
Answer: A clumsy tango can turn into this—
"BREAK" DANCING

164. **Jumbles:** CANINE STUCCO ASTHMA LAUNCH
FINISH OXYGEN
Answer: Below-zero weather means this to a veteran
weatherman—LESS THAN NOTHING

165. **Jumbles:** RATION UPSHOT ABDUCT DOUBLY
SAVORY SWIVEL
Answer: The refuse collector said his back brace was
this—A "WAIST" PRODUCT

166. **Jumbles:** THIRTY POPLAR CARBON ABLAZE
DONKEY PASTRY
Answer: Feared by many seatmates on direct flights—
A NON-STOP TALKER

167. **Jumbles:** COHORT MUSKET FLURRY BOTHER
LOCATE PENURY
Answer: What the new Cub Scouts ended up with—
A KNOTTY PROBLEM

168. **Jumbles:** HUNTER KIDNAP RARELY DEAFEN
EYEFUL OPPOSE
Answer: A vain babysitter will do this—
KEEP AN EYE ON HERSELF

169. **Jumbles:** PLENTY UNPACK LOTION COMPLY
INDUCE FEUDAL
Answer: What the chef had to do when he decided to
write a novel—COOK UP A PLOT

170. **Jumbles:** WEAPON WALLOP SNITCH CASKET
SIPHON ICEBOX
Answer: Why they asked the marksman to take the
photos—HE KNEW HOW TO SHOOT

171. **Jumbles:** COBALT ROTATE ATTAIN EYELID
SURETY ELEVEN
Answer: Why the banker offered an attractive mortgage
rate—TO CREATE INTEREST

172. **Jumbles:** CORRAL PRAYER ORIGIN JANGLE
PARADE BENIGN
Answer: Who was Tonto looking for in the bank?—
THE "LOAN ARRANGER"

173. **Jumbles:** PICKET NAPKIN CELERY BREACH
INJECT DEMURE
Answer: Often the result of an emergency tire
change—A JACKED-UP PRICE

174. **Jumbles:** COUGAR FUTILE TETHER BRUTAL
FINERY ORPHAN
Answer: What the psychiatrists turned the commuter
express into—A TRAIN OF "THOUGHT"

175. **Jumbles:** IMPUGN MELODY FROLIC ABSORB
BUREAU ALBINO
Answer: How the pasta maker increased sales—
BY USING HIS NOODLE

176. **Jumbles:** GOITER GRIMLY FUSION HEARTH
HANDED BOTTLE
Answer: They made the moonshine here—
THE "STILL" OF THE NIGHT

177. **Jumbles:** CAJOLE ROSARY TURGID HALLOW
HEALTH AVOWAL
Answer: His reason for the overcooked steak was
this—TOUGH TO SWALLOW

178. **Jumbles:** NICELY POLLEN COERCE GLANCE
ADVICE DISMAY
Answer: Easy to experience when the fish are biting—
A "REEL" GOOD DAY

179. **Jumbles:** ARCTIC PRIMER HAMPER BESTOW
BUNKER JABBER
Answer: What the young Dracula figure did to Dad on
Halloween—PUT THE BITE ON HIM

180. **Jumbles:** OPAQUE FICKLE BALSAM BICEPS
SPRUCE CANKER
Answer: College pole vaulters become this—
"UPPER" CLASSMEN

Need More Jumbles®?

Jumble® Books

More than 175 puzzles each!

Animal Jumble®
$9.95 • ISBN: 1-57243-197-0

Jammin' Jumble®
$9.95 • ISBN: 1-57243-844-4

Jumble® at Work
$9.95 • ISBN: 1-57243-147-4

Jumble® Fever
$9.95 • ISBN: 1-57243-593-3

Jumble® Fiesta
$9.95 • ISBN: 1-57243-626-3

Jumble® Fun
$9.95 • ISBN: 1-57243-379-5

Jumble® Genius
$9.95 • ISBN: 1-57243-896-7

Jumble® Grab Bag
$9.95 • ISBN: 1-57243-273-X

Jumble® Jackpot
$9.95 • ISBN: 1-57243-897-5

Jumble® Jamboree
$9.95 • ISBN: 1-57243-696-4

Jumble® Jubilee
$9.95 • ISBN: 1-57243-231-4

Jumble® Junction
$9.95 • ISBN: 1-57243-380-9

Jumble® Madness
$9.95 • ISBN: 1-892049-24-4

Jumble® Mania
$9.95 • ISBN: 1-57243-697-2

Jumble® See & Search
$9.95 • ISBN: 1-57243-549-6

Jumble® See & Search 2
$9.95 • ISBN: 1-57243-734-0

Jumble® Surprise
$9.95 • ISBN: 1-57243-320-5

Romance Jumble®
$9.95 • ISBN: 1-57243-146-6

Sports Jumble®
$9.95 • ISBN: 1-57243-113-X

Summer Fun Jumble®
$9.95 • ISBN: 1-57243-114-8

Travel Jumble®
$9.95 • ISBN: 1-57243-198-9

TV Jumble®
$9.95 • ISBN: 1-57243-461-9

Oversize Jumble® Books

More than 500 puzzles each!

Colossal Jumble®
$19.95 • ISBN: 1-57243-490-2

Generous Jumble®
$19.95 • ISBN: 1-57243-385-X

Giant Jumble®
$19.95 • ISBN: 1-57243-349-3

Gigantic Jumble®
$19.95 • ISBN: 1-57243-426-0

Jumbo Jumble®
$19.95 • ISBN: 1-57243-314-0

The Very Best of Jumble® BrainBusters
$19.95 • ISBN: 1-57243-845-2

Jumble® Crosswords™

More than 175 puzzles each!

Jumble® Crosswords™
$9.95 • ISBN: 1-57243-347-7

More Jumble® Crosswords™
$9.95 • ISBN: 1-57243-386-8

Jumble® Crosswords™ Adventure
$9.95 • ISBN: 1-57243-462-7

Jumble® Crosswords™ Challenge
$9.95 • ISBN: 1-57243-423-6

Jumble® Crosswords™ Jackpot
$9.95 • ISBN: 1-57243-615-8

Jumble® Crosswords™ Jamboree
$9.95 • ISBN: 1-57243-787-1

Jumble® BrainBusters™

More than 175 puzzles each!

Jumble® BrainBusters™
$9.95 • ISBN: 1-892049-28-7

Jumble® BrainBusters™ II
$9.95 • ISBN: 1-57243-424-4

Jumble® BrainBusters™ III
$9.95 • ISBN: 1-57243-463-5

Jumble® BrainBusters™ IV
$9.95 • ISBN: 1-57243-489-9

Jumble® BrainBusters™ 5
$9.95 • ISBN: 1-57243-548-8

Hollywood Jumble® BrainBusters™
$9.95 • ISBN: 1-57243-594-1

Jumble® BrainBusters™ Bonanza
$9.95 • ISBN: 1-57243-616-6

Boggle™ BrainBusters™
$9.95 • ISBN: 1-57243-592-5

Boggle™ BrainBusters™ 2
$9.95 • ISBN: 1-57243-788-X

Jumble® BrainBusters™ Junior
$9.95 • ISBN: 1-892049-29-5

Jumble® BrainBusters™ Junior II
$9.95 • ISBN: 1-57243-425-2

Fun in the Sun with Jumble® BrainBusters™
$9.95 • ISBN: 1-57243-733-2